DAILY DEVOTIONS

for a

GREAT LIFE

CLAUDIA WILLIAMS

WESTBOW
PRESS®
A DIVISION OF THOMAS NELSON
& ZONDERVAN

WestBow Press books may be ordered through booksellers or by contacting:

WestBow Press
A Division of Thomas Nelson & Zondervan
1663 Liberty Drive
Bloomington, IN 47403
www.westbowpress.com
1 (866) 928-1240

ISBN: 978-1-9736-9370-3 (sc)
ISBN: 978-1-9736-9371-0 (hc)
ISBN: 978-1-9736-9372-7 (e)

Library of Congress Control Number: 2020910517

Print information available on the last page.

WestBow Press rev. date: 08/06/2020

In this world, we are "salt and light" (Matthew 5:12–16). How is this concept applied to everyday life? Salt preserves and adds flavor. Flavor for life increases through the sustaining power and fullness of the Word. As salt, we deliver meaningful impact in every endeavor and with those we encounter. Light illuminates and draws others to it. With a clear vision of who God is, our lives shine as bright as the noonday sun, exuding radiance from having a deeper intimacy with Him. As salt and light, our lives are fuller and draw others to praise God. As salt and light, we experience a great life. That is God's plan.

First thing, first. The Bible instructs us to honor God with firstfruits; that applies to our money and time. Leviticus 23:10 reads, "When you come into the land which I give you and reap its harvest, then you shall bring a sheaf of the first fruits of your harvest to the priest." Immerse yourself in the captivating and loving words of God. Celebrate who He is. Show Him that He takes first place with your time. Being one with our Father is a fantastic way to start each day. Making God priority honors Him.

Reading scripture alone is not enough. Deeper reflection for applying biblical principles is necessary to move the understanding of your mind to the deeper knowing within your heart. There's a real difference between perception and knowing. Additional scripture relating to each day's topic is provided. Reading and rereading scripture instills the knowledge of God's love deep within our souls. As we reflect on the loving words of our Creator, we receive spiritual insight that invites God to walk with us on a fantastic journey into the recesses of our soul. We become enlightened through a process of expressing Biblical meaning into our uniqueness. When we put God first, He promises to tell us things that we don't know.

Reflective writing on God's Word infuses even more profound meaning and direction. Each iteration of scripture reveals a new insight and perspective. Listen to what God imparts. Write it down to gain a higher self-awareness and purpose through the spiritual examination of thoughts, feelings, and emotions. Journaling insight allows us to imagine possibilities, explore the unknown, and achieve the greatness of Biblical proportions. Journaling fosters a greater understanding of complex issues, increases creativity, and strengthens our resolve to find solutions. Regular reflective writing helps to process the emotions of life and produce greater freedom and happiness. Reading, writing, and reflecting on the application of God's word to your life, is a sacred time. Keeping a journal of Biblical insight is mysteriously good medicine for our hearts, lives, and future.

Use the *"Daily Planner for A Great Life"* alongside this devotional to organize daily priorities, as they become evident, and according to His will.

Your Character Matters

A person with a heart of stone will hurt and demoralize others. Hurting people hurt people. Excellent people encourage and build one another up. Proverbs 14:1 confirms it: "The wise woman builds her house, but with her own hands the foolish one tears hers down." Don't be misled by others of bad character. Help restore them through gentle reproof, counsel, mercy, and love. At the same time, be careful that their immoral or evil character doesn't take root in you. Make sure that you're influencing them, and that they are not impacting you.

Prayer: Lord, before I knew you, my heart was hard. I wouldn't get too close to others for fear of being hurt. But now I am a changed person. You heal, comfort, and strengthen the brokenhearted. I can love others, as you first loved me. Help me to be an excellent person, as I serve an excellent God. Amen.

Scripture for further reading: 1 Corinthians 15:33; Proverbs 12:4; Proverbs 31; Acts 17:5; Romans 5:3–5.

_____

_____

_____

_____

_____

_____

_____

Your Future

God gives a chance and a choice in life. He gives us a chance at a good life, and a choice to make it better. Jeremiah 29:11 says, "'For I know the plans I have for you,' declares the Lord, 'plans to prosper you and not harm you, plans to give you hope and a future.'" There is a saying: "Your future depends on many things, but mostly you." It's time for your destiny to be manifested. Act and pursue God's plan, the one He has planted in your heart and mind.

Prayer: Lord, help me to do my part to cooperate with your plan for my life. I can do the ordinary, but with you, I can accomplish the extraordinary. As I step out, show me the way, Lord, and help me stay alert to the promptings of my soul. Amen

Scripture for further reading: Psalm 20:4–7; 1 Chronicles 28:10–12; Colossians 3:23–25; Proverbs 16:3.

_____

_____

_____

_____

_____

_____

_____

_____

Believe in Your Dreams

The future belongs to those who keep their dreams alive. Pursue your dreams with passion. Strive towards those dreams God places in your heart. Proverbs 23:18 says, "There is surely a future hope for you, and your hope will not be cut off."

Prayer: Thank you, Lord, for placing dreams in my heart and giving me hope for the future. I am excited to see what you planned for me. Amen.

Scripture for further reading: Joel 2:28–32; Psalm 25:4–5; Isaiah 40:31; Jeremiah 29:11; Micah 7:7.

_____

_____

_____

_____

_____

_____

_____

_____

_____

_____

_____

_____

Tomorrow Is a New Day

Live one day at a time. The past is past, don't live in it — let it go. Do you wish things happened differently? Perhaps better choices could have been made. Learn from it and move on. Did you make mistakes? Learn from it and gingerly move on. Your past does not define you. What you learn from the past shapes and molds you for another day. Tomorrow is a new day. Tomorrow will be a better day. Move forward, assured by Matthew 6:25–34, which says, "Therefore I tell you, do not worry about your life. ... Can any one of you by worrying add a single hour to your life? ... your heavenly Father knows [what you need]."

Prayer: Lord, clear my cluttered mind of worry, reasoning, doubt, and confusion. I give these struggles to you and ask you to take complete control of my day, my life, and my future. Help me to maximize and enjoy each day. Amen.

Scripture for further reading: Jeremiah 31:31–34; 2 Kings 10:30; Psalm 8:4–9.

Mistakes Are Bitter, But Their Fruit Is Sweet

If you make a mistake, don't let it hold you back. Learn from it and then put it in its place — in the past. God is not finished with you yet. "He who began a good work in you will carry it on to completion" (Philippians 1:6). We are divinely blessed when we use these opportunities for greater understanding.

Prayer: Thank you, Lord, for giving me knowledge and understanding from my mistakes. People try to define me by my mistakes, but I know better. Mistakes are lessons to shape and mold me into the person you want me to be. Making mistakes is a hard but lasting way to learn the difference between right and wrong.

Scripture for further reading: Jeremiah 12:16; Daniel 1:17; Matthew 11:28–30; Leviticus 5:2–5.

_____

_____

_____

_____

_____

_____

_____

Be Safe; Be Smart

God's angels surround you. They protect and guide you. Psalm 91:11 tells us, "He will command His angels concerning you to guard you in all your ways." Take refuge in the knowledge and protection available through God's great love. God cares so deeply for those who trust in Him.

Prayer: Lord, help me see your guiding hand in the people and situations you bring into my life. You are my strength and my shield. You are my refuge, a very present help in time of need. Thank you for keeping my loved ones and me safe and protected — today and every day. Amen.

Scripture for further reading: Judges 6:12; Psalm 17:7–8; Psalm 25:20–21; Nahum 1:7; Psalm 144:2.

_____

_____

_____

_____

_____

_____

_____

_____

_____

_____

Ultimate Comfort;
Ultimate Service

There are consequences to everything that is said or done, many of which have long-term effects. Second Corinthians 1:3–4 says, "Praise be to the God and Father of our Lord Jesus Christ, the Father of compassion and the God of all comfort, who comforts us in all our troubles so that we can comfort those in any trouble with the comfort we ourselves receive from God." Comforting words and actions reflect the heart of God.

Prayer: Lord, I thank you, even when trouble surrounds me. You are there with me, in good times and bad. I put my hope in you. Thank you for comforting me through every challenge. You are my comfort and strength. May I offer solace when others are in need. May my speech be gracious, and my actions be loving. May I bring buckets of comfort, care, and smiles to those in need. Let others see you through me. Amen.

Scripture for further reading: Psalm 119:76–77; Isaiah 12:12; Isaiah 49:13; Isaiah 57:14–16.

_____

_____

_____

_____

_____

_____

_____

Share Life

Many people think that God is their errand boy. Can you imagine? The most powerful, magnificent God, an errand boy? We are here to serve God, not the other way around. First Corinthians 15:58 says, "Therefore, my dear brothers and sisters, stand firm. Let nothing move you. Always give yourselves fully to the work of the Lord, because you know that your labor in the Lord is not in vain." There are people in your community that need precisely the talent you offer. There are people in your family that need to hear a particular word of hope. God needs you to find the need and meet the need: in your home, family, church, community, and the world.

Prayer: Lord, use my hands, feet, and mouth to serve you. Help me to serve you by serving others. Amen.

Scripture for further reading: 1 Chronicles 28:20; Romans 12:3–8; 2 Corinthians 9:12–15.

_____

_____

_____

_____

_____

_____

_____

_____

Be Successful; Be Valuable

The Bible says you can serve God by serving others. Whatever your talents and gifts, God gave them to you. Are you compassionate? Loving? A go-getter? You are to use your unique gifts to help others. Galatians 6:10 says, "Therefore, as we have opportunity, let us do good to all people, especially to those who belong to the family of believers." Amen.

Prayer: Lord, thank you for the talent and opportunity to bless others. You give me opportunities to use my gifts and talents to make a difference. You give me opportunities to do what no one else is in the position to accomplish. I am purposefully placed in others' lives to make a significant impact. Thank you for trusting me to do your work. Amen.

Scripture for further reading: Genesis 12:23; Mark 12:30–31; Galatians 5:14–17; 1 Peter 4:10–11.

_____

_____

_____

_____

_____

_____

_____

_____

_____

_____

Aged to Perfection

Just as there are tests in school, there are tests in life. God allows troublesome times to test your faith in Him. Until we gain knowledge of what is divine, we are not capable of understanding what God desires. Through grace, we gain understanding, in trials, and over time. We are fallen. But through grace, we are transformed little by little and perfected into the image of Him, who is the author and finisher of faith. "[Put on] the new self, which is being renewed in knowledge in the image of [your] Creator" (Colossians 3:10). By His grace, we are aged to perfection.

Prayer: Lord, after each test, I am wiser, stronger, and more compassionate towards others who face similar challenges. Help me to pass each test and become all that you created me to be. Amid the madness, I submit to your will and grace so that I may excel in everything — in faith, speech, knowledge, and love. Amen

Scripture for further reading: Psalm 139:23–24; 1 Chronicles 28:9–10; 2 Corinthians 8:2–7.

_____

_____

_____

_____

_____

_____

_____

_____

Guard Your Heart and Guard Your Mind

God knows your heart. Your heart matters to Him. Is it full of anger or patience? Love or hate? When life happens, remember: this is a test, and you are going to pass. Tests prove what we're made of, and it's how we learn. God wants you to succeed. Guard your heart with love, kindness, forgiveness, gentleness, and patience. Guard your mind, too. The devil is always placing wrong thoughts in your head. He's been doing that since the time of Adam and Eve. Think about things of God that are noble, pure, and honorable. In Psalm 26:2 it says, "Test me, Lord, and try me, examine my heart and my mind."

Prayer: Lord, if I respond negatively to life events, help me to come up higher. Help me to react with wisdom and learn your ways. Your ways are better. Teach me your ways, Lord. Amen.

Scripture for further reading: Isaiah 55:9–13; 2 Chronicles 1:11–12; Psalm 111:10; Proverbs 3:21–26.

_____

_____

_____

_____

_____

_____

Be Committed to Godly Relations

The devil doesn't want you to love God or be in relationship with Him, or anyone else, for that matter. Try to remain at peace with God and others, as much as possible. Psalm 133:1 says, "How good and pleasant it is when God's people live together in unity." Godly relationships are a gift from God; they don't just happen —you must commit yourself to them. They are a gift from God.

Prayer: Lord, protect me from the devil's schemes to separate me from you and others. Help me restore damaged relationships and nourish the good ones. Help me to grow in godly relationships. I don't take them for granted. In Jesus' name, I pray. Amen.

Scripture for further reading: 2 Corinthians 36:12–16; Proverbs 17:17; Proverbs 18:24; Matthew 5:22–26.

Is the Devil Messing With You?

Matthew 10:22 says, "You will be hated by everyone because of me, but the one who stands firm to the end will be saved." The closer you are to God, the more the devil will mess with your life. If the devil's not messing with your life, you may need to ask yourself why. It may be because you're no threat to him or that you're not effective for God.

Prayer: Lord, remove wedges the devil places between me and others. When I am doing your work, the devil causes division, obstacles, and confusion. I also know that if I seek you, you will be with me. I am not alone. Amen.

Scripture for further reading: Matthew 13:36–43; Acts 10:37–38; Ephesians 6:11–18; Exodus 15:6.

Walk in the Light

Do you know a friend or family member walking apart from God? Being a good witness is not only what you tell them, but also what you show them. Walk in love, joy, faithfulness, goodness, peace, patience, kindness, self-discipline, and gentleness. The qualities of the Holy Spirit bring light out of darkness, joy out of sorrow, and miracles out of mayhem. Acts 1:8 says, "But you will receive power when the Holy Spirit comes on you; and you will be my witnesses in Jerusalem, and …to the ends of the earth."

Prayer: Holy Spirit, dwell in me. Help me testify to the gospel. There is no higher purpose than serving you with all that I have, with all that I am, and in everything I do. Here I am, Lord. Fulfill your purpose in me. Amen.

Scripture for further reading: Exodus 9:16; Psalm 33:10–15; Romans 8:28–30.

_____

_____

_____

_____

_____

_____

_____

_____

_____

In Pursuit of Excellence

When you reach for the stars, you may not quite get there, but you won't come up empty-handed either. Everyone has the capacity for excellence, but those who cultivate it are the ones who become genuinely useful. First Corinthians 12:31 says, "eagerly desire the greater gifts...And yet I will show you the most excellent way."

Prayer: Father, have mercy on me. I know that you put something in me that is excellent. Excellence doesn't happen by accident but is achieved with continual and gradual effort. Help me to reach inside to cultivate a spirit of excellence. I pray this in Jesus' name. Amen.

Scripture for further reading: Isaiah 48:17; Romans 9:16–18; Psalm 45:2, 1 Timothy 3:12–13.

_____

_____

_____

_____

_____

_____

_____

_____

_____

In a World of Compromise, I Won't

Not all peer pressure is bad. Sometimes learning to go with the flow is an essential part of getting along with others. It takes a person of immense character to distinguish between getting along and blindly following the crowd. "I am sending you out like sheep among wolves. Therefore be as shrewd as snakes and as innocent as doves" (Matthew 10:16).

Prayer: Father, help me make the right choices when it comes to getting along and setting limits. The world is full of compromise. Help me stand firm against making concessions that degrade or demoralize. To your glory, help me follow what is right. Give me wisdom, Lord. In your holy name, I pray. Amen.

Scripture for further reading: Proverbs 10:20–24; Philippians 1:9–11; 1 Corinthians 2:14; Galatians 4:17.

_____

_____

_____

_____

_____

_____

_____

_____

Staying Silent Never Ends Well

God has an excellent plan for your life, but you must cooperate with Him. You can't cooperate if you're rebelling. First Samuel 15:23 says, "For rebellion is like the sin of divination." We are responsible for standing up for what is right. Expressing what you think, feel, or believe is not rebellion. The trick is to disagree, agreeably. You can maintain a strong bond with others when you communicate differences without defiance. Staying silent never ends well.

Prayer: Help me, Lord, to lovingly stand for what is right. I don't want to lose or damage relations because of a difference of opinion. When appropriate, give me discernment to know when to walk away and when to speak up. Help me to stand up for what is right, even if it means I stand alone. May the seeds of patience, kindness, gentleness, and love grow and blossom within me so that your grand plan may unfold. In Jesus' name, I pray. Amen.

Scripture for further reading: Exodus 7:13–18; Acts 15:36–41; 1 Corinthians 3:3–9; Proverbs 28:14.

_____

_____

_____

_____

_____

The Enemy of Mankind

You've seen the anti-Christ. The spirit of the antichrist is anything that opposes the spirit of God or holds itself higher than God. That deceiver pours out lies to convince us to trust in what is worthless. He knows his end is coming and wants to take you right along with him. Why? He hates you because God loves you. Matthew 24:4 says, "Watch out that no one deceives you."

Prayer: Lord, I know that it's my responsibility to keep from being misled. How I spend my time and money are clues to what I value most in life. Help me to see if there is anything that I consider more important than you. If anything holds more importance than you, I am being deceived. It is through you alone that I am who I am, do what I do, and have what I have. Stay always first place in my heart, spirit, and soul. In Jesus' name, I pray. Amen.

Scripture for further reading: Exodus 20:5–6; Deuteronomy 26:10–11; Isaiah 44:6–8; Job 15:31.

_____

_____

_____

_____

_____

_____

_____

Spirit of Praise

There are times in everyone's life that it seems the whole world is coming against them. During these times, the Bible says to put on "a garment of praise instead of a spirit of despair" (Isaiah 61:3). Write down some good things in your life — there's always something good. Consider colors, birds, sunshine, and shelter; what beautiful gifts we take for granted. Being thankful turns things around.

Prayer: Thank you for being who you are, Lord. You are a great and mighty God, a gentle and kind Comforter, Redeemer, and Savior. Thank you for the goodness of each day, including the air I breathe and the kindness of a stranger. May I start each day praising your Holy Name. Help me end each day the same way — thanking you for your many blessings. I come to you, Father, with praise and thanksgiving. In Jesus' name, I pray. Amen.

Scripture for further reading: Genesis 24:26–27; Deuteronomy 8:10–11; Psalm 13:3–6; Psalm 30:9–12; Psalm 67:3–5.

Flames of Envy

Does a friend or neighbor own what you've been hoping for? That's not a coincidence. If you can be happy for them, that opens the door for God to bring that same blessing to you. God desires to bless you, but bitterness and envy stop the flow of blessings. James 3:14 says, "But if you harbor bitter envy and selfish ambition in your hearts, do not boast about it or deny the truth." These feelings are not of God but are earthly, unspiritual, and from the devil.

Prayer: God, I confess that I get a twinge of envy when someone has something that I desperately desire. Help me to replace these feelings with happiness for them. Then I can be secure knowing that through continued faith, blessings will also be available for me. Amen.

Scripture for further reading: Job 5:2–4; Proverbs 14:30; Proverbs 23:17–18; Galatians 5:16–26.

Boundless Confidence

Confidence is a feeling that comes with emotional security, and knowing who you are in Christ. You gain confidence in yourself by keeping a positive attitude, having values to live by, and making sacrifices to accomplish your dreams. "For the Lord will be at your side and will keep your foot from being snared" (Proverbs 3:26). Christians, come boldly before God's throne of grace, knowing we may receive mercy and find grace to help in every need. This confidence blesses us.

Prayer: Lord, as I abide in you, and you abide in me, I am fully confident, knowing that I am in your will. Knowing that I am one with you gives me the confidence to step out in faith towards accomplishing my dreams. Thank you, Lord Jesus. Amen.

Scripture for further reading: Psalm 71:5–8; Jeremiah 17:7–8; 2 Thessalonians 3:4–5; Hebrews 4:16.

_____

_____

_____

_____

_____

_____

_____

_____

Play Your Part

Everyone has different gifts. Some people are talented with their hands, others with knowledge. Second Corinthians 9:6–7 says, "Remember this: Whoever sows sparingly will also reap sparingly, and whoever sows generously will also reap generously. Each of you should give what you have decided in your heart to give, not reluctantly or under compulsion, for God loves a cheerful giver." Christians often misunderstand this message, believing they are to give until it hurts. That's not God's intention, as He longs for your happiness. It's joyful to give. Giving is a good thing and brings joy to others, and you receive a blessing in the process. But when the pleasure in giving is gone, pay attention. The season for giving might be over. Likewise, a season of giving may come to an end when you feel compelled to give out of guilt or shame. Also, giving should be curtailed when it's not appreciated. When you feel your very life is being sucked away from you, it is a sign that the season of giving is done. God doesn't want you living someone else's life. You are responsible for living your life, and others are accountable for living their life. If you feel used and degraded, it's time to turn your attention to other areas God may be calling you. Don't stop giving, but be guided by the promptings of the Holy Spirit.

Prayer: Father, you gave me a spirit of giving. You blessed me with abundance to share with others. There is always something I can do to make someone's day better — a smile, a kind word, a gift, a hand. Help me to be a better giver. And likewise, help me discern when and where my talent best serves your purposes. In Jesus' name, I pray. Amen

Scripture for further reading: Psalm 119:93–96; Proverbs 11:17–18; Luke 11:42; Acts 20:32–35.

Pure Heart

Many of faith, fall short of God's glory. They limit the infinite favor and blessing of God by not practicing what they know to be true. Forgiving others is a requirement. We often deceive ourselves, believing we are forgiving but continue to harbor ill feelings and resentment. How often do you pray that God will love those who hurt you? Have you ever vented to others about someone's offense? Matthew 5:8 says, "Blessed are the pure in heart, for they will see God." Only those who are blameless and pure in heart will experience God's perfect will and good favor.

Prayer: Lord, give me a pure heart. As much as I can bear, reveal to me my iniquities. Once I understand hidden areas of my heart that hinder my relationship with the Holy Spirit, I will give an account for any impure thought, feeling, emotion, or action. Forgive me, Lord, if there is any anger, envy, jealousy, bitterness, or unclean thing in me. Restore in me the innocence of a child. Give me a pure heart. In Jesus' name, I pray. Amen.

Scripture for further reading: Proverbs 22:19; 1 Timothy 1:5–7; Ephesians 5:3–10.

Don't Miss God

Many Christians encourage others to join their religion instead of leading them to Christ. Jesus detested Pharisees, who were so religious. They were so religious, and they missed Jesus. They were so worried about traditions and laws that they didn't recognize who He was. They were so arrogant and judgmental, and they crucified Him. Don't miss Him. "For I tell you that unless your righteousness surpasses that of the Pharisees and the teachers of the law, you will certainly not enter the Kingdom of Heaven" (Matthew 5:20).

Prayer: Lord, the most beautiful blessing of life is the fullness that comes from a life spent with you. Time in your presence is peace, joy, hope, and love. Time in your presence is refreshment for the soul. Who wouldn't want that? I pray to spend more time in your presence each day, on purpose. In Jesus' name, I pray. Amen.

Scripture for further reading: Psalm 51:10–12; Psalm 89:15–18; Jude 1:24–25.

Happiness Is a Choice

It's easy to get discouraged about everything that's going on in the world today. But there is a choice in how you respond. Happiness is a choice. People are going to be as happy as they make up their minds to be. There is always something to be joyful about. Look for God's goodness, on purpose, and celebrate it. When discouragement creeps in, immediately replace those thoughts, feelings, and emotions with words of life. "The joy of the Lord is [my] strength" (Nehemiah 8:10).

Prayer: Lord, the Serenity Prayer, ascribed to Reinhold Niebuhr, defines wisdom in response to out-of-control situations. It reads, "God grant me the serenity to accept the things I cannot change, the courage to change the things I can, and the wisdom to know the difference." Help me Lord to let go of things that I have no control over, and to pursue peace and joy. Help me let go of anything that keeps me from experiencing the joy and happiness you richly provide and intend for me. In Jesus' name, I pray. Amen.

Scripture for further reading: Deuteronomy 30:19–20; Ecclesiastes 2:26; Matthew 25:21.

Offense Is an Ego Problem

Some people like to nurse and rehearse offense. Let go of it. The offense is designed to make you hold a grudge against others instead of loving them. The attack makes you give up on people when you should be helping them. Offense keeps you from receiving abundant blessings that would otherwise be yours. "There is no one righteous, not even one" (Romans 3:10).

Prayer: Lord, give me the grace to let go of offense. I make mistakes too. No one is perfect. We're all on this journey, called life. Help me to release offense quickly and forgive others. Help me realize that those who hurt me probably didn't intend to. Those who hurt me are themselves deeply troubled and in need of compassion. In your holy name, I pray. Amen.

Scripture for further reading: Proverbs 17:9; 1 Kings 8:47–51; Ezekiel 18:30–32.

_____

_____

_____

_____

_____

_____

_____

_____

_____

_____

Keeping Family Together

Take a stick and break it. It's easy to do. Now try to break a bundle of sticks tied together — it's not going to happen. That's what family, Christians, and friends need to do — stick together. Colossians 3:13 commands us to "Bear with each other and forgive one another if any of you has a grievance against someone. Forgive as the Lord forgave you." A single stick is easily broken, but not so with a bundle.

Prayer: Lord, it's easier to forgive my child than others when harsh words are spoken. Because of my deep love for my child, I am more willing to understand, correct, and comfort. I would do well to give strangers more consideration. Help me to cover every offense with love, as much as possible, knowing there's more to gain in remaining in unity. Amen.

Scripture for further reading: 2 Chronicles 30:12; Psalm 133:1; Ephesians 1:9–10; Ephesians 4:3.

_____

_____

_____

_____

_____

_____

_____

_____

Self-Discipline

Self-discipline will help you accomplish more than skill alone, ever can. Self-discipline makes you practice and work harder. Just because you acquire a profession or ability does not mean that you will apply it. If you want your share of the reward, you must take your share of the work. Proverbs 12:1 says, "Whoever loves discipline loves knowledge, but whoever hates correction is stupid."

Prayer: Lord, I appreciate things more when I work for them. It's easy to take things for granted if they come easy or naturally. Hard work, dedication, and stick-to-itiveness make me appreciate the goal once I've achieved it. Help me learn discipline Lord, so that I may go after the goal. Amen.

Scripture for further reading: 1 Corinthians 9:24–27; 2 Timothy 1:7; Titus 1:7–9.

_____

_____

_____

_____

_____

_____

_____

_____

Complaining

Do you ever wonder why it takes so long for God to answer prayers? There may be a straightforward answer. The Israelites spent forty years traveling an eleven-day journey to the promised land. Why? Rather than thanking and praising God for his goodness, they complained non-stop. Negativity is like a damp, drizzly day to the soul. How do you feel listening to negative, complaining, whiny people? Constant complaining gets old. Do you feel inclined to lend an ear to moaners and groaners? Do you jump in and fix their problems? Wouldn't you rather hear a compliment than a criticism? It's more pleasant to be with people who are cheerful and positive. God is no different. The Bible gives examples of ungrateful, grumbling, and complaining people throughout the old and new testaments. First Peter 4:9 suggests, "Offer hospitality to one another without grumbling."

Prayer: Lord, I come to your throne of grace with praise and thanksgiving. Change my voice Lord from grumbling and complaining to rejoicing and praising. In Jesus' name, I pray. Amen.

Scripture for further reading: Numbers 11:1–3; Ezra 3:10–13; Psalm 100:1–5.

_____

_____

_____

_____

_____

_____

Know the Bible

Spend time reading the Bible. The Bible is God's love letter to humankind. In James 1:18, we are reminded of our value in the eyes of the King of kings, which says, "He chose to give us birth through the word of truth, that we might be a kind of first fruits of all he created." His words are life and intended for our well-being.

Prayer: God, I cherish the love shown through every word in the Bible. Your word is a blessing to me, a guide for me, and a light within me. Guide my family and me with your love away from harm and direct us on the right path. Amen.

Scripture for further reading: 1 Peter 4:11; 1 John 2:5–6; Revelation 22:18–20.

_____

_____

_____

_____

_____

_____

_____

_____

God's Word Is Power

God's word is power. The Bible was written by men, but inspired by God. God gave us the word for dominion over all situations. God's word overcomes temptation, purifies our hearts, quiets our minds, and provides spiritual nourishment. Matthew 4:4 reminds us that "Man shall not live on bread alone, but on every word that comes from the mouth of God."

Prayer: Father, thank you for your word. Help me spend time reading and meditating on it. The answer to every problem is found in your word. It is truth, wisdom, and power. Help me to share it with others. In Jesus' name, Amen.

Scripture for further reading: Hebrews 1:1–4; John 6:67–69; Proverbs 30:5–6.

_____

_____

_____

_____

_____

_____

_____

_____

_____

A Compass in Life

The Bible is a compass for life. God's word terrifies the devil. Receive the promise of Joshua 1:8, which says, "Keep this book of the law always on your lips; meditate on it day and night, so that you may be careful to do everything written in it. Then you will be prosperous and successful."

Prayer: God, your Word gives life, builds faith, and brings miracles. It creates change, alters conditions, and triumphs over adversity. Your Word instills hope, develops character, and imparts joy. Your Word guarantees my future forever. Amen.

Scripture for further reading: Psalm 1:2–6; Psalm 119:15–16; Psalm 119:27–32.

_____

_____

_____

_____

_____

_____

_____

_____

_____

_____

_____

_____

Looking to God for Answers

Many people look to others for answers when they're afraid. They don't know to combat fear with faith. The Bible reminds us in 1 Peter 5:7 to "Cast all your anxiety on Him because He cares for you." What freedom there is knowing that the Father, Almighty God, is taking care of you. He's in control. He's got you covered.

Prayer: God, each time a need arises, I will seek your wisdom and strength. Help me find faith to fight every fear. Instead of relying on my job, the government, or others to provide for me, I am reminded to seek provision from you. You, God, are the source of all I need. Amen.

Scripture for further reading: 2 Samuel 22:29–33; Daniel 2:20–23; Matthew 11:28–30.

_____

_____

_____

_____

_____

_____

_____

_____

_____

My Mantra

Find a phrase in the Bible that helps you. Repeat the sentence in your mind, say it out loud, write it down, and read it over and over, until it is rooted deep within your heart. As you meditate on the phrase, make it your mantra. One of my favorite mantras says, "Take delight in the Lord, and He will give you the desires of your heart" (Psalm 37:4). Matthew 11:28 is beneficial when you're feeling overwhelmed: "Come to me, all you who are weary and burdened, and I will give you rest."

Prayer: Thank you, Father that your Word is refreshment for my soul. For every situation or challenge I face, and every burden I carry, you have provided a way. Amen.

Scripture for further reading: Jeremiah 31:25; Psalm 23:3; Proverbs 3:7–8.

Real Strength

Are there areas of life where you are weak? Celebrate them. God has promised in 2 Corinthians 12:9, "My grace is sufficient for you, for my power is made perfect in weakness." I am not a good cook, yet God gave me a daughter who is a good cook. I can celebrate and appreciate her talent. My husband is a disciplinarian; I am more compassionate. Together, we balance one another's strengths and weaknesses. Because of our limitations, we can see and appreciate God's glory in other people. Another way His power is made perfect in our weakness, is in making the seemingly impossible possible, so that we may witness His glory.

Prayer: God, you allow areas of weakness in my life to remind me to depend on you. Demonstrate your power in me. Lord, you are my strength and my song. You are my joy and hope. In Jesus' holy name, I pray. Amen.

Scripture for further reading: Isaiah 12:2–6; Romans 8:1–5; 2 Corinthians 4:7–12; Exodus 35:30–36:1.

It Is All for Gain

God allows weakness, for there is purpose in it. Deficiency increases ones' capacity for compassion. Lack causes us to fall on our knees in desperation, and rely exclusively on God. As we push through, despite our weaknesses, we gain knowledge. Once delivered from our limitations and deficiencies, we gain a testimony to share with others. We can comfort others with knowledge of the promise found in Philippians 4:13, which says, "I can do all [things] through Him who gives me strength." The next time you feel inadequate, remember that, with God, it is all for gain.

Prayer: Lord, I know that no one is perfect. Condemnation of weakness, in ourselves or others, is demeaning and detrimental to the life within us. It doesn't make anything better. Instead, help me, Lord, to show compassion and encourage others to walk through this time and hold their heads high, knowing that you are walking with them. Amen.

Scripture for further reading: Acts 11:23–24; Romans 1:11–12; Romans 15:5–6; 1 Thessalonians 3:7–9.

Greatness in Me

Many people think of themselves as human beings having a spiritual experience, but that's not the case. The truth is, we are all spiritual beings in human form. First John 4:4 says, "You, dear children, are from God and have overcome them because the one who is in you is greater than the one who is in the world." Amazing! The Creator of the universe, full of majesty and splendor, is alive within each one of us. In Him, we have the spirit of greatness.

Prayer: Father, may I be less self-serving, self-indulgent, and self-glorifying. May I be God-centered so that the life, love, and power in me will produce supernatural results. May the fullness of your glory live within me. Amen.

Scripture for further reading: 2 Corinthians 13:5; Galatians 2:20; Ephesians 3:14–19; Colossians 1:27.

_____

_____

_____

_____

_____

_____

_____

_____

Serve God by Serving Others

You can serve God by serving others. You weren't created just to consume resources — to eat, breathe, and take up space. God designed you to make a difference. What God told Jeremiah is also right for us. "Before I formed you in the womb, I knew you, before you were born, I set you apart. I appointed you as a prophet to the nations" (Jeremiah 1:5). God predestined you for His particular purpose; to make a difference now and into eternity.

Prayer: Lord, I am in awe of you. When I think about the work to do on this earth today, I feel humbled and inadequate. I am a vessel chosen by you to love others, speak into their lives, and share the ever-present hope in knowing you. Use me, Lord, to accomplish your amazing purpose. Amen.

Scripture for further reading: 1 Chronicles 29:15–19; Psalm 62:10–12; Joshua 24:14–15.

_____

_____

_____

_____

_____

_____

_____

_____

_____

Christ in Me

Anyone who is only concerned about himself, and does not love others should seriously consider whether Christ lives in them. People who use their God-given abilities to help others are fulfilling their calling. God asks us to take all that we are, and use it for His eternal purpose. Don't you know making a difference in someone's life not only helps them but those around them? Adding to one person's life has a lasting impact on future generations. At the end of life, everyone will stand before God and give an account of their commitment to sharing their talents, opportunities, and gifts. Whatever gifts and talents Christ placed within you, use them to sow into the lives of others.

Prayer: When my time comes, God, I pray to hear you say, "Well done, good and faithful servant. You have been faithful with a few things; I will put you in charge of many things. Come and share your master's happiness" (Matthew 25:21). It is an enormous privilege to be one with you, Lord, and do your will. Give me the heart to sow into the lives of others. Amen.

Scripture for further reading: Matthew 25:21; 2 Timothy 1:9–14; 2 Timothy 3:10–17.

_____

_____

_____

_____

_____

_____

Victory Over Fear

Fear stands for False Evidence Appearing Real. Fear is the opposite of faith. Faith is based on believing in what is not seen. Faith in our Father is what He demands from us. Deuteronomy 31:6 says, "Be strong and courageous. Do not be afraid or terrified…for the Lord your God goes with you; He will never leave you nor forsake you." Don't focus on your fear, but on your Father in Heaven. Worship Him. That is where the victory lies.

Prayer: Help me, Lord, to replace fear with faith. Help me to realize that you are with me in all situations. You are an omnipotent God; I ask for the faith of a child to trust you more. Amen.

Scripture for further reading: Hebrews 2:11–15; Romans 15:13; 1 John 5:1–15.

_____

_____

_____

_____

_____

_____

_____

_____

_____

Compassion

Ephesians 4:32 says, "Be kind and compassionate to one another, forgiving each other, just as in Christ God forgave you." Having compassion for others is like offering them a precious gift. Forgiving is a gift for you. Forgiveness releases you from the prison of inner turmoil that gives others power over your emotions and behavior. Forgiving doesn't require reconciliation or that you concur. Forgiving means that through compassion for their weakness, their errors, and their injustice, you can turn the matter over to God and let Him do what only He can do. Then, you can move forward, living the abundant life God called you to.

Prayer: Lord, you suffered many things, including rejection, abuse, and false accusations. Yet on the cross, you gave us unmerited mercy and grace. Help me to be a light in this dark world by offering compassion. Give me compassion to provide comfort, strength, forgiveness, guidance, and reassurance to others. Help me move forward in all the joy and fullness of life you prepared for me. I can do this because you first did this for me. Thanks be to you, God. Amen.

Scripture for further reading: Ephesians 4:32; Isaiah 30:18; Isaiah 2:3; Deuteronomy 30:1–10.

_____

_____

_____

_____

_____

_____

Religious Superficiality

Jesus did not like the Pharisees – they were legalistic religious people. Some people find security in laws and rules, and either knowingly or unknowingly, use legalism to control and manipulate the conduct of others. Similarly, some Christians today are more concerned with political correctness or moral obligations than they are in having a relationship with the King of kings, the Lord of lords, the Great I Am. Paul spoke harshly about the religious Pharisees when he wrote: "As for those agitators, I wish they would go the whole way and emasculate themselves" (Galatians 5:12).

Prayer: I pray Lord to grow nearer to you each day. You promised that you would draw nearer to us, as we draw nearer to you. Fan the flame of my desire to draw closer to you. As for me and my house, I pray that you will open the door of our hearts and minds and abide in us. Forgive me for focusing on appearances, rules, and traditions of religion. I pray for a deeper and more intimate relationship with you. Make my life a sweet reflection of the hope, love, and joy available through you. In Jesus' name, I pray. Amen.

Scripture for further reading: John 5:39; 1 Kings 8:59–61; Ecclesiastes 5:1; James 4:8; Matthew 16:6–12.

But for the Grace of God

"For it is by grace you have been saved, through faith — and this is not from yourselves, it is the gift of God — not by works, so that no one can boast. For we are God's handiwork, created in Christ Jesus to do good works, which God prepared in advance for us to do" (Ephesians 2:8–10). When we consider those less fortunate, we are reminded of the saying, "But for the grace of God, there go I." Grace alone keeps us from having a very different kind of life. Be thankful for your good fortune. By God's grace, we are blessed with opportunities and gifts. Grace is the greatest gift given freely by God.

Prayer: Father, you have showered me with infinite gifts. I am humbled and amazed by your grace, Lord. Thank you for your saving grace. Amen.

Scripture for further reading: Acts 20:32; Romans 3:22–26; Romans 5:1–2; James 4:10.

You Are Set Free

Do you know anyone who will not let you forget your mistakes? God forgets your errors and turns them into good for your sake. Romans 6:14–22 says, "For sin shall no longer be your master, because you are not under the law, but under grace. What then? Shall we sin because we are not under law but under grace? By no means. But thanks be to God. You have been set free from sin …so now offer yourselves as slaves to righteousness leading to holiness…and the result is eternal life." We all sin, but when we know the love of the Father, we desire to turn away from sin and sin no more. He knows our weaknesses. He knows our infirmities. Through God's amazing grace, we are not condemned but guided to better ways.

Prayer: Lord, thank you for your forgiveness and saving grace. Because of your sacrifice, I am no longer a slave to sin, but thirst for righteousness. I feel deep sorrow for my sins. I am passionately devoted to you because of your undying love. Help me to turn from sin, be kept from temptation, and choose to live my life according to your abundant blessings. In your precious name, I pray. Amen.

Scripture for further reading: Psalm 142:7; Romans 3:22–26; 1 Corinthians 1:26–31; 1 John 1:5–10.

_____

_____

_____

_____

_____

Attitude Is Everything

Your life is what your thoughts create. Keep a positive attitude. Jesus sets high standards for us in this area. "As the heavens are higher than the earth, so are my ways higher than your ways and my thoughts than your thoughts" (Isaiah 55:9). Stay positive by replacing negative thoughts and attitudes with the promises of the Bible. When self-defeating thoughts creep in, replace them with the prevailing mantra, "I am chosen." If feelings of shame and guilt slither into the dark crevasses of your mind, know that they are not from our heavenly Father. You are made right by the blood of Jesus. Declare, "I am a victor and not a victim" over oppression. Feeling rejected? Look in the mirror and remind yourself, "The King of kings loves me." Depression has no place in your life. Take authority over the enemy. You are fearfully and wonderfully made. You are more than a conqueror. Take authority over your thoughts and attitudes.

Prayer: Lord, I am the gatekeeper of my thoughts. Help me to interrupt fearful or wrong thoughts and feelings. I know those wrong thoughts prevent me from moving forward into the victorious life you prepared for me. Help me to declare the promises found throughout the Bible. Thank you, Father. Amen.

Scripture for further reading: Philippians 4:8; Romans 15:5–6; Hebrews 4:12–13.

_____

_____

_____

_____

_____

Plan for My Life

What God has planned for your life, may not coincide with your plans. God's plan is richer. His plan is better than anything you could hope or imagine. To experience the fullness of God's plan, you must first know Him. Not just about Him, but know Him personally. You must know who you are in Him. You must be honest with God about who you truly are, including your strengths, weaknesses, wants, and wishes. Before you experience God's abundant plan, you must abide in Him and He in you. How else will you know His will? As you walk with the Holy Spirit, ask for guidance, follow peace, and pay attention to the opportunities and circumstances around you. They are not coincidences. Romans 8:28 says, "And we know that in all things God works for the good of those who love Him, who have been called according to his purpose."

Prayer: Lord, thank you for creating a purpose and plan for my life. Help me to follow the prompting of the Holy Spirit to achieve the dreams placed on my heart. Give me proper and well-balanced priorities. Help me to stay centered in your will. Help me to be all that you created me to be. In Jesus' name, I pray. Amen.

Scripture for further reading: Isaiah 46:9–11; Ephesians 1:11; Proverbs 19:21; Matthew 6:33; Matthew 19:26.

_____

_____

_____

_____

_____

Guilt Is a Lie

Satan will always try to make you feel guilty. That's not what God wants. The journey to holiness is not without mistakes and imperfection. When you make mistakes, be patient with yourself. God's not finished with you yet. If you cooperate with Him, you will, like a fine wine, get better and better with age. First John 1:9 says, "If we confess our sins, [Jesus] is faithful and just and will forgive us our sins and purify us from all unrighteousness."

Prayer: Lord, when I make mistakes, you promise that if I confess my faults, I will be forgiven and changed. It's hard to admit my faults. Things that I hide, or am blind to, have power over me. Anything that keeps me from being my best, Lord, reveal it to me and remove it from me, so that it no longer possesses power over me. Thank you for the miracle of confession. A pure heart is pleasant for the soul. A clean conscience is nourishment for the soul. A joyful spirit is sweet. Thank you, Lord, for the privilege of coming to you in prayer. Amen.

Scripture for further reading: Ezekiel 18:30–32; Psalm 25:6–11; Psalm 119:132–136; Proverbs 28:13–14.

_____

_____

_____

_____

_____

_____

_____

The Devil Will Lie to You

Don't believe the first thing that pops into your head. The devil will tell you, "You should have done better," or "You messed up." The devil tries to convince you that you are lacking, but it is a lie. Stay rooted in the Word. Find the joy that God has promised. "Those who seek the Lord lack no good thing" (Psalm 34:10).

Prayer: Lord, to stop wrong thoughts, help me immediately replace them with promises in the Bible. Help me to speak up, speak out, and proclaim what you said about me. I am chosen, cherished, and blessed. I am loved. Dear Lord, abolish every evil scheme, every lie, and every attack of the enemy against me, my family, and loved ones. In the name of Jesus, I pray. Amen.

Scripture for further reading: Psalm 37:30–34; 2 Thessalonians 2:16; Luke 15:21–24.

Isn't Everyone Spiritual?

God created everyone, but not everyone is a child of God. Do you know someone spiritual, who doesn't know God? There exists a spiritual dimension in the world where people witness spiritual experiences that are not of God. There is also a secular spirituality promoting personal growth and inner peace, which likewise does not include the divinity of our Heavenly Father. Any spirit that doesn't confess that Jesus is God is a spirit of the antichrist (1 John4:1–3). We are instructed to test spirits and false prophets. God has given us the privilege of being born again so that we are now members of His family. God is such a gentleman that He will not force Himself on us. He gives us a choice to receive His love and mercy. Hebrews 11:6 says, "And without faith, it is impossible to please God because anyone who comes to Him must believe that He exists and that He rewards those who earnestly seek Him."

Prayer: Lord, may I seek you diligently every day. I know the road is wide to destruction, but I choose the path of your righteousness for your name's sake. Help me to discern what is true and right. I choose to receive you. Amen.

Scripture for further reading: 1 John 4:1–3; Proverbs 2:20–22; Proverbs 4:1–27; Isaiah 26:7–9; Ephesians 5:8–10.

_____

_____

_____

_____

_____

Body of Christ

When you turn your life over to God, what do you receive? The Bible promises you will be with God forever. You will become like Christ. In Heaven, there will be no pain, death, or suffering. You will be rewarded and reassigned positions of service. "Therefore, you do not lack any spiritual gift as you eagerly wait for our Lord Jesus Christ to be revealed" (1 Corinthians 1:7).

Prayer: Lord, don't let me miss the promises you made for those who choose to serve and honor you. Reveal your glory Lord Jesus to my loved ones and me. May we never be separated from you. Amen.

Scripture for further reading: Romans 8:28; 1 Samuel 26:23–24; Hebrews 11:6.

_____

_____

_____

_____

_____

_____

_____

_____

_____

Self-Inflicted

I want a friend who will make me happy. I want parents with enough money to buy lots of stuff for me, and I want a car that suits me. It's all about me. Self-centeredness is the religion of our time. Do you know anyone who seems to have it all, and is still unhappy? Full of bitterness? Wrought with judgment? The Bible says, "Whoever wants to become great among you must be your servant, and whoever wants to be first must be your slave — just as the Son of Man did not come to be served, but to serve, and to give his life as a ransom for many" (Matthew 20:26–28). Happiness is more than being blessed; It's about being blessed so much that you can bless others. There are so many ways to be a blessing to others. Find yours.

Prayer: Today, Lord, what I want is to serve you. I want to be a friend, a helper, a caregiver, and a disciple. Amen.

Scripture for further reading: Proverbs 28:26; Luke 12:15–21; 1 Timothy 3:13.

God's Will

When I was a child, I wanted to be a clockmaker. While I admire that trade, I would be lousy at it. My hands aren't steady, and I want to get things done quickly. Sometimes I get ideas about what I want to do, but God knows best. God is the potter. The clay can't tell the potter, "I want to be a vase," or "Shape me tomorrow." In Jeremiah 18, the potter shapes and reshapes the clay until it takes a form that pleases Him. The Israelites, for whom this passage was written, expected God to serve them instead of them serving God. But because of the stubbornness of their evil hearts, they continued with their plans. They missed the great opportunity before them and suffered God's wrath. God is on the throne and wants to create a beautiful vessel in you. Let God be God of your life.

Prayer: Lord, mold me and make me. Help me turn the will of my life over to you. I want to live the life you chose for me. Amen.

Scripture for further reading: Isaiah 45:9–10; Jeremiah 18:1–10; 1 Timothy 6:11–19; 1 John 2:15–17.

_____

_____

_____

_____

_____

_____

_____

Life Before Jesus

When I was a teenager, I kept looking for someone to rescue me, to understand me, to love me. I thought I could fulfill these needs through family, friends, or others. What I got was anything but fulfilling. I did not find the answer to what I was looking for until I made Jesus my Savior. People are human and will disappoint you — even good people. It was when I began to seek Jesus that I found the greatest joy ever known. James 4:8 confirms it: "Come near to God, and He will come near to you. Wash your hands, you sinners, and purify your hearts, you double-minded."

Prayer: Father, I long for love, peace, joy, hope, faith, kindness, and goodness. Father, help me not to look to others for what I can only receive from you. Free me from any darkness in my heart. I welcome your generous and fulfilling love. Amen.

Scripture for further reading: 1 Thessalonians 5:4–11; Philippians 3:7–14; Mark 5:19.

Take a Chance

Sometimes we get too comfortable with the status quo. We get set in our ways and don't want to change. I don't know who first said this, but please give them significant recognition for their wisdom, which says, "If you want something different, you must be willing to do something you've never tried before." You can't keep doing the same thing and hope for different results. The scripture from Isaiah 55:11 suggests that "My word… will not return to me empty, but will accomplish what I desire and achieve the purpose for which I sent it." To achieve a goal, see it, say it, and do something in faith to make it happen.

Prayer: God, grant me the courage, strength, wisdom, and faith to reach for the goal and do what is necessary to achieve it. Lord, help me not be captured within my comfort zone. I long for the life you desire for me. Amen.

Scripture for further reading: Proverbs 6:6–11; Proverbs 21:5; Proverbs 16:9.

Focus

Obstacles are those annoying occurrences that happen when you take your eyes off the goal. Learn to prioritize. Life is short. Don't waste time on things that don't matter. Spend time on things that make a difference for eternity. Philippians 3:14 says, "I press on toward the goal to win the prize for which God has called me heavenward in Christ Jesus."

Prayer: Lord, help me to be a good steward of the resources you've entrusted to me. I pray for the resolve to manage, with wisdom, and go after the prize. May my time, energy, and money be used to make a difference for your heavenly kingdom. Amen.

Scripture for further reading: Romans 12:2; Proverbs 24:27; Colossians 3:23; 1 Corinthians 9:24–27.

The Choice Is Yours

Life happens. There's no choice about what life brings your way. The only option available is how to respond. A positive response is like a spark that ignites fireworks — extraordinary things happen. "A person finds joy in giving an apt reply — and how good is a timely word" (Proverbs 15:23).

Prayer: Lord, I know how powerful words can be. You created the universe by speaking it into existence. You gave us the Bible so that we can speak power into any seemingly uncontrollable circumstance. Help me to know the Bible better and speak powerfully over people and situations. I pray this in Jesus' name. Amen.

Scripture for further reading: Luke 6:45; 1 Peter 3:9; Proverbs 11:17; Proverbs 18:1.

_____

_____

_____

_____

_____

_____

_____

_____

_____

The Power of Attitude

Life is not controlled by what happens; life is controlled by ones' attitude. Attitude shapes your thoughts, behavior, and character. "The Lord detests the thoughts of the wicked, but gracious words are pure in His sight" (Proverbs 15:26). It all starts with attitude; whether positive or negative, people respond accordingly. You impact the outlook of those within your circle of influence. Have you ever thought about how your attitude influences others? A positive attitude sees the challenge as an opportunity; a negative attitude observes the same situation and sees defeat.

Prayer: Lord, I know that a positive attitude is that little thing that makes a big difference. Whatever my perspective, it has an impact on my mood for the day, and the quality of interaction with others. Living with a positive outlook leads to the fulfillment of expectations for good. Giving me a choice in attitude is the power you've given me to shape the events of my life. Please help me in every situation, remember that the attitude I choose has significance. Thank you, Lord. Amen.

Scripture for further reading: Colossians 3:10–15; Psalm 34:8–9; Psalm 25:3–5; Romans 12:2.

_____

_____

_____

_____

_____

_____

The Spirit of Determination

You were created for a reason, and when you realize that reason is something that must be achieved, you gain confidence and determination. Then you can go after the goal despite the obstacles you face. "I cry out to God Most High, to God who vindicates me" (Psalm 57:2). The God who is within you is greater than any challenge.

Prayer: Lord, I open my mouth and proclaim that I am your child, and you are my God. You are pleased with me. I am no surprise to you. You know my mistakes. You know where I am headed. Your plans for me are good because you are good. Thank you, Lord Jesus. Amen.

Scripture for further reading: 1 Corinthians 16:13; James 1:12; Joshua 1:9; 2 Chronicles 20:17.

_____

_____

_____

_____

_____

_____

_____

_____

_____

The Essence of Change

The Greek philosopher Heraclitus said, "Everything changes but change itself." Indeed, life is continually changing, but every change has its purpose. Learn to embrace change. "He changes times and seasons; He deposes kings and raises up others. He gives wisdom to the wise and knowledge to the discerning" (Daniel 2:21).

Prayer: Thank you, Lord, for changing circumstances. Thank you, Lord, for changing me. While all change seems difficult at the time, I can know with certainty that good will come out of it. Help me to focus less on the undesirable aspects of change and trust you will use it for good for those who love and seek you. I can rest knowing that you are in control, and this grim season will pass. I praise you for your goodness. Amen.

Scripture for further reading: Thessalonians 5:18; Ecclesiastes 3:1; Jeremiah 29:11; Ezra 10:4.

Life Is a Journey

Life is a journey to learn how to live. Until you spread your wings, you'll never know how far and how high you can fly. Open your mind and your heart to the fullness of God's grace and all that He would like to do for you. "May the God of hope fill you with all joy and peace as you trust in Him, so that you may overflow with hope by the power of the Holy Spirit" (Romans 15:13).

Prayer: With you, God, all things are possible. Because of your grace Lord, I find joy in the journey, discovering that I am a prosperous, whole, and healthy creation. To you be all the glory. Amen.

Scripture for further reading: Hebrews 11:7; Genesis 12:1–2; Philippians 1:6; 2 Peter 3:18.

_____

_____

_____

_____

_____

_____

_____

_____

_____

Pay Attention to the Finer Details

Achieve excellence by paying attention to the finer details. "Finally, brothers, whatever is true, whatever is noble, whatever is right, whatever is pure, whatever is lovely, whatever is admirable — if anything is excellent or praiseworthy — think about such things" (Philippians 4:8). Anyone who climbs the ladder of success, finishes their race, or reaches the top of the highest mountain, yet treats others rudely in the process, has missed the finer details. Completing the goal is not as crucial as the process of getting there. God cares about the finer details,

Prayer: Lord, help me live each day with excellence. Help me be aware of the finer details that matter most to you. Help me be committed to the process. Let me reach my destination with excellence. In Jesus' name, I pray. Amen.

Scripture for further reading: 1 Corinthians 12:31–13:3; 1 Timothy 3:13; Titus 3:1–8.

_____

_____

_____

_____

_____

_____

Opportunity

There is a century-old saying, "Opportunity knocks but once." The wisdom of this idiom is that success comes to those prepared for each opportunity. The Bible tells us, "Ask and it will be given to you; seek, and you will find; knock, and the door will be opened to you" (Matthew 7:7–8). Christians, excuses will always be there, but opportunity won't. When the opportunity comes, go after it.

Prayer: Lord, when I was young, I found myself standing at a stranger's door, knocking to ask for money for a fundraiser. I was afraid they would reject me. Lord, I don't want to miss any opportunity you provide me. Help me to unclench my tight fist knocking at the door, and be ready to accept the prospect beyond the open door. Amen.

Scripture for further reading: Matthew 7:7–11; 1 Corinthians 16:5–9; Revelations 3:19–20.

_____

_____

_____

_____

_____

_____

_____

_____

How Many Lives Have You Touched?

A hundred years from now, it won't matter how much money you had, what kind of house you lived in, or how many cars you owned. What will matter is how many lives you touched. First John 4:7 reminds us, "Dear friends, let us love one another, for love comes from God. Everyone who loves has been born of God and knows God." Love is the instrument that God richly provided for us to fulfill His purpose in bringing others into His eternal and glorious presence.

Prayer: Lord, when I think about my purpose on earth, there is nothing more valuable than touching others' lives for you. Soften my hardened heart to love others in a way that will glorify you. Help me to demonstrate the same love, mercy, joy, hope, compassion, and encouragement you provide me. May others see you in me. In Jesus' name, I pray. Amen.

Scripture for further reading: Luke 18:10–14; 1 Corinthians 9:19–23; Colossians 4:2–6.

Teamwork

Teamwork is the ability to work together with one heart. Achieving more requires diligent cooperation with others. Synergy is created by dividing the task and doubling the success. The letters in the word team stand for together, everyone, achieves, more. We continually see examples in the Bible of how we are to work with one another. "If you see your fellow Israelite's donkey or ox fallen on the road, do not ignore it. Help the owner get it to its feet" (Deuteronomy 22:4).

Prayer: Lord, I don't want to be a glory hound, insisting on doing things by myself. Help me to work more collaboratively with others to accomplish greater success. Help me celebrate the gifts of others. Let me encourage others to do more, see more, and be all that you intended them to be. Help us use the synergy of teamwork to do amazing things for your glory. Amen.

Scripture for further reading: Colossians 3:13–14; Psalm 133:1; 1 John 4:12; Galatians 3:26–28.

Thinking Outside of the Box

Imagine the unimaginable. Make possible what seems impossible. "So we fix our eyes not on what is seen, but on what is unseen since what is seen is temporary, but what is unseen is eternal" (2 Corinthians 4:18). Billy Graham was a simple man with a purpose larger than himself. Mother Teresa was small in stature, but the magnitude of her mission was magnificent. People who have accomplished the unimaginable focused on things outside themselves, outside their abilities. With the help of the Holy Spirit, they ministered to dignitaries, and their message of God's love spread throughout the world. Because they reached beyond themselves, they brought massive amounts of people to God, making an eternal difference for the Kingdom of God.

Prayer: Lord, help me think outside the box so that with the Holy Spirit, I can accomplish more. Help me to use more resources, access what's beyond my capabilities, and get outside my comfort zone so that I experience the extraordinary events awaiting me. Amen.

Scripture for further reading: Matthew 19:26; Mark 11:24; Jeremiah 32:17.

_____

_____

_____

_____

_____

_____

Never Accept Mediocrity

Never accept mediocrity. The joy found in the pursuit of excellence is a mysterious thing. Dream bigger, work harder and be dedicated to the task at hand. "You are the most excellent of men, and your lips have been anointed with grace since God has blessed you forever" (Psalm 45:2). Walking in the ways of God brings joy and perfection.

Prayer: Bless me, Lord, and create excellence within me. With your help, I will move forward with big dreams, always remembering to find joy and peace in the process. Help me always to seek you first and give you the glory. Help me to act with kindness and gentleness toward everyone, and to love and be kind to others in the process. Amen.

Scripture for further reading: Mark 9:23; Philippians 4:13; Hebrews 12:1; Isaiah 40:31.

_____

_____

_____

_____

_____

_____

_____

_____

_____

Someone Who Understands Me

God understands your needs. You can tell Him anything and everything that you hope and dream for. While He already knows what you want before you ask, He wants to be a part of your every day hoping and dreaming. "If you believe, you will receive whatever you ask for in prayer" (Matthew 21:22). God in heaven is a Father who wants to bless you, but He'll never give you more than you can handle. You can't give your five-year-old the keys to the Maserati. Nor can your Heavenly Father give you the keys to all the treasures and joys of your heart until you're ready for them. Make Him a part of your hoping and dreaming and seek His wisdom and understanding in the process. God wants this kind of relationship with you. Get ready for blessings.

Prayer: Lord, be a part of every area of my life. Give me the wisdom and understanding to care about what's important to you. Help me to value what you value. Help me to walk with you and be worthy of blessing and favor. Come into my life, Lord Jesus. Amen.

Scripture for further reading: Proverbs 4:6; Colossians 2:2; Psalm 139:1–6; James 1:5–8; James 3:13; John 15:16.

_____

_____

_____

_____

_____

Draw Closer to the Throne of Grace

"If you remain in me and my words remain in you, ask whatever you wish, and it will be done for you" (John 15:7). It is easy to feel spiritual on Sunday in church. Drawing closer to the throne of grace becomes more challenging during the week. Rushing to balance home and family commitments while, at the same time, pursuing success in a demanding job seem to consume all the time and energy we have. Take Him with you into the day, and your heart will be at peace. Do everything throughout the day, unto God. See the blessing in all of it. From the smallest chores to the most rewarding/challenging event of the day, God is there. Listen to worship music, pray throughout the day, and ask to be led by the Holy Spirit. Remain in Him. Make God part of your everyday life.

Prayer: Lord, be with me on Sunday, Monday, Tuesday, Wednesday, Thursday, Friday, and Saturday. Be with me while driving to work, paying bills, and preparing dinner. Be with me today as I make small decisions and life-changing decisions. Be in my heart, home, and future. May I abide in you and you in me. In Jesus' name, I pray. Amen.

Scripture for further reading: John 15:15; James 4:8; Revelations 3:20; Proverbs 3:5–6; Proverbs 22:11.

_____

_____

_____

_____

_____

He Fights My Battles

During life's battles, it's easy to be discouraged. In the strife, it's challenging to know what direction to take. Emotions in conflict are intense. Struggles are wrought with confusion and chaos. Knowing that trials build character, strengthen resolve, and make us stronger, give little comfort in the fray. But knowing that the King of kings is there through life's most difficult times is enough. He fights your battles. First Samuel 17:47 says, "All those gathered here will know that it is not by sword or spear that the Lord saves; for the battle is the Lord's." Turn your cares over to the Lord.

Prayer: Lord, give me faith in trials, for I know that pleases you. Faith in the battle releases me from the shadows of fear and worry. You are my vindicator. I shall have no fear. In Jesus' name. Amen.

Scripture for further reading: Romans 5:3–5; James 1:2–4; Romans 8:17–18; James 1:12.

A Grateful Heart Finds Many Blessings

If you asked me what I was thankful for right this second, I would produce a very long list. I'm grateful for my dog, who makes me laugh. I'm grateful for the warm sunshine on my skin. I'm thankful for my family and friends. I'm grateful for the ocean breeze and the flocks of birds that fly south for the winter. I'm just thankful. I am blessed with more than I could ever hope or imagine. "Let the peace of Christ rule in your hearts, since as members of one body you were called to peace. And be thankful" (Colossians 3:15).

Prayer: God, Let me take time to see the good. Let me enjoy and celebrate all that you provide. I am thankful and praise your holy name. Amen.

Scripture for further reading: Colossians 3:15–17; 1 Thessalonians 5:18; Ephesians 5:20; Psalm 100:4.

_____

_____

_____

_____

_____

_____

_____

Relax and Enjoy

Know that God personally guides you on this journey, called life. Knowing that God is in control and has great plans for your life makes the journey enjoyable. Proverbs 3:5–6 tells us to "Trust in the Lord with all your heart; and lean not on your own understanding; in all thy ways submit to Him, and He will make your paths straight."

Prayer: God, as I go through the day, make your presence known to me. You are watching over me, walking with me, and pouring your love in me. There is so much joy and peace in knowing you are with me. Amen.

Scripture for further reading: Matthew 28:18–20; Isaiah 41:10; Luke 12:22–26.

_____

_____

_____

_____

_____

_____

_____

_____

_____

Your Highest Priority

Get your priorities straight. Make your family a high priority, but keep God in the first place. It is God who gives you family. Matthew 10:37 reminds us, "Anyone who loves their father or mother more than me is not worthy of me; anyone who loves their son or daughter more than me is not worthy of me." This passage reminds us to put Christ first, and God will take care of the rest.

Prayer: Lord, when I place you at the center of my life, I am assured that you provide all that I need. I ask for the correct attitude, perspective, boundaries, and motives to reflect a knowing that you are the best gift of my life. May I be an example to others who desperately need you, of the hope and love that is available in you. Give me a godly home and life. Amen.

Scripture for further reading: Matthew 6:31–33; John 3:30–36; Luke 12:28–31; Deuteronomy 6:5.

Work Harder; Play Longer

Do your utmost in the work you're assigned. Achieve success with hard work, enthusiasm, and continuous commitment. Balance that passion and drive with a good quality of life. Exodus 20:9 says, "six days you shall labor and do all your work." Too much work or too much play can create stress. Everything in moderation is vital.

Prayer: Lord, it is good to work hard and rest. You allow us to experience joy in accomplishing our goals. You also want us to rest, rejuvenate, and be refreshed. Your plan is good. Thank you for your balance: you give us the strength, ability, and courage to succeed, and you provide us with rest to enjoy it. Amen.

Scripture for further reading: Proverbs 18:9; Genesis 2:2–3; Exodus 20:11; Proverbs 8:30–31.

_____

_____

_____

_____

_____

_____

_____

_____

Good Company

It's essential to surround yourself with people who are good company. People rub off on you. When you surround yourself with people who complain, you tend to be negative. When you associate with people who are motivating, you get encouraged. Likewise, people form opinions about you based on the character of your friends. First Corinthians 5:11 says, "But now I am writing to you that you must not associate with anyone who claims to be a brother or sister but is sexually immoral or greedy, an idolater or slanderer, a drunkard or swindler. Do not even eat with such people."

Prayer: Lord, I ask that you send godly friends of good character. May I support others by encouraging them through everyday challenges, and share the hope of walking closer to you each day. I pray this in your name. Amen.

Scripture for further reading: Proverbs 13:20; Proverbs 22:24–25; Colossians 3:12–14; Ecclesiastes 4:9–10,

You Are Worthy

Don't try to prove your worth to anyone. Know that you are worthy because you are a child of God. "For you are a people holy to the Lord your God. The Lord, your God, has chosen you out of all the peoples on the face of the earth to be his people, his treasured possession" (Deuteronomy 7:6). Know that you are loved and of great value to the Lord your God.

Prayer: Lord, of all the beautiful experiences I had with you today, I wonder which was the best. Was it the fragrant smell of flowers, the precious child that made me laugh, or was it the beautiful day, that stirred the greatest joy within my soul? I never want to overlook these incredible kindnesses from you or the extent of your love for me. Amen.

Scripture for further reading: 1 Peter 2:9; Deuteronomy 14:2; Jeremiah 1:5; Ephesians 1:3–4.

_____

_____

_____

_____

_____

_____

_____

_____

_____

When Life Doesn't Feel Right

Wrong thoughts prevent us from experiencing the presence of the King of Glory. So too, associating with evil people, plans, and activities keep us from experiencing the joy and loving presence of God. Genesis 6:5 says, "The Lord saw how great the wickedness of the human race had become on the earth, and that every inclination of the thoughts of the human heart was only evil all the time." God wants so much to demonstrate His glory. He wants so much to reveal His power and love. The enemy will always try to block the flow of God's great goodness by putting the wrong thoughts in your head. Here's how to defeat the enemy's scheme and allow God's blessings to flow into your life: replace negative thoughts with positive ones.

Prayer: Lord, when life doesn't feel right, remind me to repeat this as a mantra, "Surely your goodness and love will follow me all the days of my life, and I will dwell in the house of the Lord forever" (Psalm 23:6). Amen.

Scripture for further reading: Romans 8:28; Psalm 103:1–5; 1 Peter 5:6–7.

_____

_____

_____

_____

_____

_____

_____

How Can I Hear From God?

When you pray, don't do all the talking. With a pure heart, be still, and invite the Holy Spirit into your life. Earnestly seeking God and desiring wholeheartedly to follow His teachings will produce rewards; bring awareness to the indwelling of the Holy Spirit. Just be aware of His presence and pay attention to that small voice within. First Corinthians 6:19 says, "Do you not know that your bodies are temples of the Holy Spirit, who is in you, whom you have received from God? You are not your own."

Prayer: If there is any unclean thing in my heart, forgive me Lord and wash me clean, so that I may come before you and be a witness to your glory. What peace, joy, and splendor reside, from sitting still with the great I Am. You are with me and know my every thought, care, and need. Teach me your ways, Lord. In Jesus' name, I pray. Amen.

Scripture for further reading: Jeremiah 33:3; John 7:17; John 8:47; John 14:26; Psalm 119:105–112; Romans 10:17.

_____

_____

_____

_____

_____

_____

_____

How to Pray for Others

If you are praying for someone else, know that God has a solution to every problem. His answer is always the best way. We may not understand God's way, but He has promised that everything occurs for the ultimate good for those who love Him. Hold your friend or loved one's problems up to God. See the vision of God surrounding them in His great mercy and love. Imagine God shining His perfect, pure, and holy will on them. "[A servant of Christ Jesus] is always wrestling in prayer for you, that you may stand firm in all the will of God, mature and fully assured" (Colossians 4:12).

Prayer: I ask to pray powerfully for my friends and loved ones. I pray that you are with them now in their time of need, holding them, healing them, and restoring them. I stand firm in the knowledge that you want only your best for them and in you, the victory is already won. Praise be to you, God. Amen.

Scripture for further reading: Romans 8:26–27; James 5:13–16; Ephesians 6:10–18.

_____

_____

_____

_____

_____

_____

_____

Be Wise

Proverbs speaks of wisdom and folly — both are portrayed as gifts. Satan, the great deceiver, makes folly appealing, to keep you from walking after Jesus. He also promotes the easy way, half-truths, and lies to keep you from finding the wisdom offered by God. Satan is loud, and his advice is free. But God is a gentleman and will not force Himself on you. Proverbs 28:26 tells us, "Those who trust in themselves are fools, but those who walk in wisdom are kept safe." Seek the truth through the word of God.

Prayer: Father, may I forever walk in the wisdom found in your word. Your ways are higher. Your ways are better. Cover me with the word and victory found in your name. Amen.

Scripture for further reading: 2 Corinthians 22:10–11; Revelations 12:7–12; Matthew 7:15–29; John 10:10.

_____

_____

_____

_____

_____

_____

_____

_____

_____

Purpose for Everything

Why do bad things happen to good people? When you ask yourself this question, stop. Trust God and know there is a purpose for everything. "There is a time for everything, and a season for every activity under the heavens: a time to be born and a time to die, a time to plant and a time to uproot, a time to kill and a time to heal, a time to tear down and a time to build, a time to weep and a time to laugh, a time to mourn and a time to dance, a time to scatter stones and a time to gather them, a time to embrace and a time to refrain from embracing, a time to search and a time to give up, a time to keep and a time to throw away, a time to tear and a time to mend, a time to be silent and a time to speak, a time to love and a time to hate, a time for war and a time for peace" (Ecclesiastes 3:1–8). We don't need to know all the answers, but we know the one who does. Knowing and trusting in His perfect timing and will is enough.

Prayer: Lord, I don't need to understand different seasons in life, but I ask for wisdom to remain faithful through them all. Remind me to trust you. I ask for your covering over my life. You work all things for good, for those who know, love, and serve you. Thank you, Lord, Jesus. Amen.

Scripture for further reading: Jeremiah 29:11; Jeremiah 32:19; Proverbs 16:4; Romans 8:28.

Walk in Confidence

What happens when you let doubt rule your thoughts and actions? James 1:6 says, "But when you ask, you must believe and not doubt, because the one who doubts is like a wave of the sea, blown and tossed by the wind." Because the Holy Spirit is alive, you can walk in confidence. Cast down wrong thoughts and fill your mind, heart, and soul with the hope, promise, and faith you have in Jesus.

Prayer: Lord, you are God of the universe, with unlimited power and infinite resources. Forgive me when I walk in doubt. Help me to go forward always in confidence, knowing you are on the throne of my life, and that you work all things for good, for those who diligently seek you. Thank you, Lord Jesus, Amen.

Scripture for further reading: Genesis 6:5–9; Psalm 10:4–7; Mark 7:20–23; Psalm 13:2–8.

Believing Versus Knowing

It takes practice to get better in sports. Workouts and competition make us stronger. It's the same with life. God allows struggles to make us stronger and create greatness within us. Philippians 1:27–30 says, "Whatever happens, conduct yourselves in a manner worthy of the gospel of Christ. Then, whether I come and see you or only hear about you, stand firm in one Spirit, striving together as one for the faith of the gospel without being frightened in any way by those who oppose you." When trials come, stand firm, and stand with other believers without being afraid. Practice makes perfect.

Prayer: Well, Lord, there's no doubt about it, I'm going to need your help today. When challenges come, I know you are with me. I know that I can stand firm in my faith without being frightened by the opposition. I know trials will come, and without any doubt, you are creating greatness in me. This knowledge surpasses a hopeful belief and allows me to meet any challenge with confidence. This knowing has prepared me for such a time as this. Thank you, Lord Jesus, for the confidence I have because of you. Amen.

Scripture for further reading: Esther 4:13–14; Isaiah 61:3; Ephesians 6:10–17; 1 John 5:18.

Divine Struggles

If you are going through struggles, know that difficult times are just as divine as good times. In the book of Job, an innocent man suffered greatly. Satan had challenged God to a contest on earth. Would Job turn against God and lose his faith if his life were destroyed? Sometimes, our lives seem to be a mess. God seems to be distant and silent. Job's confidence in the rock-solid sovereignty of God, provides an example for us during difficult times. "Though he slay me, yet will I hope in Him; I will surely defend my ways to His face" (Job 13:15).

Prayer: Father, help me to remain as reverent as Job during difficult times. Being reverent in difficult times doesn't mean I need to acquiesce, but instead, demonstrate that you are the priority of my life. When life's struggles become so large, I can't fix them on my own. Help me to seek you Lord to do what only you can do. I affirm your absolute sovereignty and trust that my victory can be found alone in you. Amen.

Scripture for further reading: 1 Peter 5:8; Psalm 28:7; Psalm 37:5; 2 Corinthians 12:9–10; 1 Corinthians 10:13.

MARCH 25

Pressure From Others

There will be people who try to persuade you to act or think the way they do. Develop a strong sense of who you are, because you will be tested. Psalm 12:2–3 says, "Everyone lies to their neighbor; they flatter with their lips but harbor deception in their hearts. May the Lord silence all flattering lips and every boastful tongue." Words can do tremendous good or evil. Guard your heart against ways that are not of God.

Prayer: Lord, keep me from being deceived. When others try to deceive me, help me to replace trust in what others say, with faith in what the Bible says. Help me to know the Bible better, listen for your voice, and follow you. Amen.

Scripture for further reading: Romans 12:2; Galatians 1:10; Proverbs 1:10; Acts 5:29.

_____

_____

_____

_____

_____

_____

_____

_____

_____

_____

Peace and Prosperity

Experience peace in the presence of God. You can find peace in every situation. It is a choice to make. You don't need to fix a condition to be at peace. The stronger your faith in God, the more peace you will experience. "Submit to God and be at peace with Him; in this way, prosperity will come to you" (Job 22:21).

Prayer: Lord, I know control is an illusion, and when I spend time trying to make things happen, the result is prideful manipulation. There is undeniable peace when I turn my cares over to you. May I submit to you and walk in peace in every situation. Amen.

Scripture for further reading: Job 22:21; Matthew 11:28–30; Isaiah 26:12.

_____

_____

_____

_____

_____

_____

_____

_____

_____

A Personal Relationship With God

In silence, you will hear the voice of God. When Jesus prayed, He "went off to a solitary place" (Mark 1:35). When you find a quiet place and shut out all thoughts and distractions, focus on the Holy Spirit within. When you do, you will come into direct contact with the loving presence of God.

Prayer: Spending time in your holy presence, Father, I experience the peace that surpasses all understanding. I feel inner joy, love, and beauty. Thank you for the privilege of experiencing the inner sanctuary that comes from being in your presence and having a personal relationship with you. There is nothing like it to compare. Amen.

Scripture for further reading: John 14:23; Psalm 16:11; Psalm 27:4; Psalm 65:4; 2 Corinthians 3:12–18; Hebrews 9:1–9.

Are You an Ego Maniac?

The ego is an exaggerated belief in one's superiority. To get a good indication of how massive your ego is, think about the number of times a day, you use the word "I." Romans 12:3 reminds us, "Do not think of yourself more highly than you ought, but rather think of yourself with sober judgment, in accordance with the measure of faith God has distributed to each of you." Lucifer's elevated ego was the reason our adversary was hurled out of the Kingdom of God forever. Pride, arrogance, and the desire for self-recognition hardened his heart. As a result of pride, Lucifer was separated from the love, peace, and joy of God forever. Praise God for any goodness He has conferred to you. Give God the glory.

Prayer: Lord, my confidence and self-assurance come from knowing that I am the child of the most loving God Almighty. Help me tame my ego. All glory and honor are yours, heavenly Father. Amen.

Scripture for further reading: John 5:30–32; 1 Peter 5:5; Proverbs 16:5; Ephesians 3:12; Hebrews 14:16.

Pride Goes Before the Fall

The ego is a subtle adversary. Don't take credit for your talents, accomplishments, or character, when the glory alone belongs to our Lord. The ego is a powerful self-destruct mechanism. It works through pride, but as we know, pride comes before the fall. Habakkuk 2:4 states, "See, the enemy is puffed up; his desires are not upright — but the righteous person will live by his faithfulness."

Prayer: Father, thank you for the skills, opportunities, talents, and accomplishments you so graciously provide. May I replace any self-centeredness with God-centered love. Remind me to give you the glory, rather than taking credit for what is rightly yours. I give you thanks for all that I am and all that I hope to be. In Jesus' name, I pray. Amen.

Scripture for further reading: 1 Corinthians 10:31; Revelations 4:11; 2 Peter 1:3.

_____

_____

_____

_____

_____

_____

_____

_____

Listening to Others

Listen twice as much as you speak. Listening is an essential element of an empowered future. Proverbs 15:31 says, "Whoever heeds life-giving correction will be at home among the wise." Wisdom is freely available to those who stop talking and start listening.

Prayer: Father, you gave me two ears and one mouth. I should listen twice as much as I speak. You shower me with affection, attention, and devotion. I pray to give others this same consideration. Help me to listen to their ideas, their concerns, and their affairs. Help me, Father, to be a better listener. Amen.

Scripture for further reading: Proverbs 1:5; Proverbs18:13; Proverbs 19:27; Psalm 34:11; Job 34:2–4; Isaiah 42:20–23.

_____

_____

_____

_____

_____

_____

_____

_____

_____

Healing Is in the Tongue

When you meet a friend, listen to them before you start going on about yourself. When you focus on your friend's feelings, you'll know how to respond to them. When you listen to others, really listen, you'll be more sensitive and choose your words more carefully. Words are powerful. They can destroy people or build them up. Words can save a friend from making wrong choices or encourage them to do good works. "The tongue that brings healing is a tree of life, but a deceitful tongue crushes the spirit" (Proverbs 15:4).

Prayer: Lord, I ask to know the right words to bring healing, comfort, wisdom, peace, and strength. In every thought, word, and deed, lead me to the bright and loving light of your kingdom. Teach me to bring light into this dark world. In Jesus' name, I pray. Amen.

Scripture for further reading: Psalm 37:30–31; Psalm 49:1–3; Psalm 145:3–13; Isaiah 33:15–16; Jeremiah 6:10.

Releasing Inner Turmoil

"A person's wisdom yields patience; it is to one's glory to overlook an offense" (Proverbs 19:11). When someone has offended you, let it go. Will your being offended change anything? More than likely, the other person had no intention of hurting you. Often, each offense has more to do with your expectations, rather than anything said or done. Besides, when you continue to hold a grudge, you are allowing them to control your emotions. Keep a journal of the offenses against you. Sometimes writing them down helps you vent and release the inner turmoil that would otherwise cause hurt relations, ruin your day, or fester into something bigger.

Prayer: Lord, I know that it delights the devil when he stirs up adversity, when we are offended, when we hold grudges, and when we let ill-feelings boil up inside of us. Letting go of offense is your will for me so that I can focus more on the good in life. Help me to forgive so that I can be released from a prison of inner turmoil. In Jesus' name, I pray. Amen.

Scripture for further reading: Psalm 129:2–4; Mark 5:34; 2 Samuel 22:47–50.

_____

_____

_____

_____

_____

_____

Service Is a Precious Commodity

My mother always told me, "Give more of yourself and ask less in return." Give your time to help lift the sweet spirit of a child or take flowers to an elderly neighbor who's shut-in. In Matthew 25:40, Jesus said, "Truly I tell you, whatever you did for one of the least of these brothers and sisters of mine, you did for me."

Prayer: Lord, I can show love, compassion, and peace because that is what you pour out on me. Help me to be a better steward of the resources you've given me, and use them to help those in need. It is a blessing to help others. Thank you for trusting me to do your good work. Amen.

Scripture for further reading: 2 Chronicles 31:20–21; Titus 3:4–8; 1 Peter 4:10–11.

Authentic Happiness

Do you ever think, "If I just had that job or that car, I'd be happy?" True happiness doesn't come from having or getting things. Whatever your God-given talents and gifts, share them freely with those who could benefit. Do you bake cakes? Make one for someone who needs their spirit lifted. "To the man who pleases Him, God gives wisdom, knowledge, and happiness, but to the sinner, he gives the task of gathering and storing up wealth to hand it over to the one who pleases God" (Ecclesiastes 2:26).

Prayer: Lasting joy doesn't come from having, getting, or taking care of myself. Jesus, my joy is in you, and in doing your will. May my joy be complete in you. Amen.

Scripture for further reading: Philippians 2:1–8; 1 John 1:1–4; 2 Chronicles 9:7–8.

_____

_____

_____

_____

_____

_____

_____

_____

_____

Keep the Main Thing, the Main Thing

The Bible tells us that "[we] must turn from evil and do good; [we] must seek peace and pursue it" (1 Peter 3:11). How do we pursue it, find it, and walk in it? We choose peace by dwelling with God. Rise early to spend time with Him. Walk with Him throughout your day. Celebrate every blessing with Him. Lean on Him in every trial. When we maintain peace during trials, it thwarts, troubles, and torments the devil. God desires our freedom, found through peace.

Prayer: Lord, let me experience the peace that comes from knowing you personally. Let my primary motivation for life be to know and follow you — not morality, work, family time, evangelism, principles, disciplines, or even church. Help me keep the main thing, the main thing — to experience the peace found in a more meaningful relationship with you. Amen.

Scripture for further reading: Romans 1:7; Philippians 4:7; 2 John 1:3.

_____

_____

_____

_____

_____

_____

Peace in Our Relationships

Philippians 2:3 says, "Do nothing out of selfish ambition or vain conceit. Rather, in humility value others above yourselves, not looking to your own interests but each of you to the interests of the others." Never take good relationships for granted. Too many times, one incident or one bad day can change the course of a friendship. Friendships will be tested. Be patient during such times. Don't insist on having your way; instead, treat one another with respect.

Prayer: Lord, it's hard to understand why there's struggle in relationships, but I know you are teaching me something I desperately need. As I walk with others through this world, I need your help to treat others as I would like to be treated. Help me to understand more than I insist on being understood. Stay near to me, Lord Jesus. Amen.

Scripture for further reading: 2 Corinthians 1:12–14; Colossians 3:15–17; Matthew 7:12; 1 Samuel 20:42.

An Enemy Called Pride

Don't consider yourself more important than anyone else. Regard others as a gift. Regard others as the prize that they are in your life. Proverbs 11:2 says that "when pride comes, then comes disgrace, but with humility comes wisdom." The work God assigns to one person is equally important as the work assigned to others. There is an Italian proverb that reminds us that after a game of chess, all the pieces go back into the same box. Similarly, at the end of our lives, we all stand before our King, on judgment day. Two things are important for every God-given assignment. First, do everything to the best of your ability, and second, treat everyone as equal and necessary players in the game of life.

Prayer: God, thank you for trusting me with my part in this game of life. Help me to treat others as essential to the success of every endeavor. We're all in it to win it. God of grace, help us work together collectively using the gifts and talents given to each one of us, to finish our assignment successfully, and better than we could individually. Amen.

Scripture for further reading: Acts 6:8–10; Deuteronomy 8:10–14; Psalm 101:5–6.

Sometimes the Devil Will Give You Something Good, to Keep You From God's Best

"And this is my prayer: that your love may abound more and more in knowledge and depth of insight so that you may be able to discern what is best and may be pure and blameless for the day of Christ" (Philippians 1:9–10). Sometimes the devil will give you good things to keep you from God's best. Talk to God about your commitments. Make commitments only to things that bring inner peace. Learning to say "No" to those things that create stress, yields less anxiety, and greater fulfillment.

Prayer: Lord, all too often, I underestimate the deliberate evil strategies of the devil to derail me from your plan. I accept things because they satisfy my selfish desires or because of a sense of obligation. Whatever the reason, help me to fight for the superior joy found in following peace. Help me to rely on the still small voice that brings inner peace to know the better way. Amen.

Scripture for further reading: Luke 8:11–15; 10:39–42; 1 Peter 5:8–11.

_____

_____

_____

_____

_____

_____

Self

There is a fine line between self-esteem and self-centeredness. Self-esteem comes from hard-work, sincerity, and success. People with high self-esteem are a pleasure to be around. Self-centeredness is the result of thinking that the world revolves around me, and the misconception that I am better than everyone else. Self-centered people are not a pleasure to be around. Romans 12:16 says, "Live in harmony with one another. Do not be proud, but be willing to associate with people of low position. Do not be conceited."

Prayer: Lord, you give us two arms, two legs, a heart, a mind, two eyes, two ears, and one mouth – all are necessary for me to accomplish what I need to do. So, it is with life. We need others, and everyone needs to do their part to achieve the goal. All are necessary; all are important; all need to work together. You showed us this Lord as you sought fellowship with your disciples. Help me to live in harmony with others. Help me to replace any self-centeredness with self-esteem. Amen.

Scripture for further reading: Matthew 9:38; Proverbs 27:17; Matthew 4:18–22.

Pure and Peaceful Heart

Do you ever insist on getting what you want, when you want it? Peace doesn't come from having your way. Peace and harmony don't just come to you — you must work for it. First Peter 3:8 says, "Finally, all of you, be like-minded, be sympathetic, love one another, be compassionate, and humble."

Prayer: Lord, I believe that the heroes of this world are those who pursue peace. Help me to renounce the culprits that steal my peace, which are anger, sorrow, resentment, frustration, and jealousy. I pray Lord to pursue a pure and peaceful heart. Amen.

Scripture for further reading: Psalm 17:3–8; Psalm 26:2–7; Colossians 3:15–19.

As Much as Possible, Be at Peace With Everyone

There will always be people who irritate you, hurt you, or annoy you. Getting them out of your life is not the answer. God has allowed them in your life to do a good work in you. Perhaps He is using them to teach you forgiveness, patience, compassion, or some other shortcoming. What do you do? Discover how your character will grow by having known them. "Turn from evil and do good; seek peace and pursue it" (Psalm 34:14). Seek to understand God's purpose in every situation, in every relationship, and remain at peace.

Prayer: Lord, I know that you are more interested in developing my character, than in making me comfortable. Thank you for the people and situations you bring into my life. None of them are a coincidence. Thank you for loving me enough to change me from glory to glory to glory. Amen.

Scripture for further reading: Romans 5:1–5; 2 Corinthians 1:12–14; 2 Timothy 2:22–26.

_____

_____

_____

_____

_____

_____

Busyness

If the devil can't make you bad, he'll make you busy. Being in a hurry and overwhelmed will rob you of your peace. If you feel overwhelmed, pray about it before you decide whether something should be done, delayed, delegated, or deleted from your schedule. Philippians 4:6 says, "Do not be anxious about anything but in every situation, by prayer and petition, with thanksgiving, present your requests to God."

Prayer: Lord, thank you for being so accessible. Help me slow down and know that you are with me. Help me to create space in my life and know where to set proper boundaries. With more freedom of space and time, I can be the best version of myself. Guide me to focus on your will in my life each day. In Jesus' name, I pray. Amen.

Scripture for further reading: Psalm 46:10–11; Matthew 25:14–30; Ephesians 4:1; 1 Peter 1:17–25.

_____

_____

_____

_____

_____

_____

_____

_____

Self-Acceptance

There is peace in self-acceptance. You may not be where you want to be in life, but God loves you so much, He will help you get where you need to be. The Bible says in 2 Corinthians 5:21, "God made Him who had no sin to be sin for us so that in Him, we might become the righteousness of God." In God's eyes, you are holy, perfect, and righteous. He knows your past, present, and future, and He still loves you unconditionally. He won't give up on you. The one who counts the most loves you. If God thinks you're great, just accept it.

Prayer: Lord, help me to replace negative emotions with Biblical truths. Remind me that you love me, and you love me just the way I am. Thank you, Lord Jesus. Amen.

Scripture for further reading: John 16:27; 1 Chronicles 11:28–32; Psalm 136:1–3.

_____

_____

_____

_____

_____

_____

_____

_____

Build One Another Up

Make a difference in this dark world. Show sincere support, thoughtfulness, and encouragement to those who may feel unappreciated or mistreated. Sharing the right word at the right time may help a friend believe in themselves, reach their full potential, or pursue their greatest dreams. Listen, share, inspire, and give them hope. Romans 14:19 says, "Let us therefore make every effort to do what leads to peace and to mutual edification."

Prayer: Lord, a friend is a gift from you. Lead me to godly friends. We all need encouragement from time to time. Help me to be the kind of friend I'd like to have. Help me to be a light in this dark world. Help me to build others up. Amen.

Scripture for further reading: Philippians 2:1–7; 1 Corinthians 12:26; Ephesians 4:32; 1 Peter 3:8.

APRIL 14

There Is Power in Words

Sticks and stones will break my bones, but words will never hurt me. As a child, you probably professed that saying, but it certainly is not valid. Poorly chosen words ruin relationships. Words can cause pain or pleasure, anger or peace, frustration or contentment, and loneliness or wholeness. The Bible teaches us that "The soothing tongue is a tree of life, but a perverse tongue crushes the spirit" (Proverbs 15:4).

Prayer: Lord, you created me to be a speaking spirit in your image. You created the universe by speaking into it. The Bible is proof of the power of words. It is a weapon to protect and provide supernatural power. Help me to choose my words carefully. Amen.

Scripture for further reading: Genesis 1:1–27; Exodus 4:11–12; John 33:14–18; Hebrews 4:12–13.

_____

_____

_____

_____

_____

_____

_____

_____

_____

You Get What You Give

People tend to judge one another during the first few minutes they meet. What do your words, appearance, and body language tell others about you? If you give your best, people will be inclined to provide you with nothing less. Colossians 4:6 says, "Let your conversation be always full of grace, seasoned with salt, so that you may know how to answer everyone."

Prayer: Lord, I pray to reflect your character in all relationships. Help me always to choose words that are full of grace. Holy Spirit, use this message to encourage and empower me to make my conversations full of grace and seasoned with salt. Help me, Lord, to know how to answer everyone. Amen.

Scripture for further reading: Psalm 19:1–6; Numbers 23:19–20; Deuteronomy 32:1–4; Psalm 19:14.

_____

_____

_____

_____

_____

_____

_____

_____

_____

Practice Peace

When conflicts arise, it is human nature to either run or attack. A better solution is to make peace. Peace brings honor to God and benefits everyone involved. "So, whether you eat or drink or whatever you do, do it all for the glory of God. Do not cause anyone to stumble, whether Jews, Greeks, or the church of God — even as I try to please everyone in every way. For I am not seeking my good but the good of many, so that they may be saved. Follow my example, as I follow the example of Christ" (1 Corinthians 10:31–11:1). What a different world this would be if we all practiced peace.

Prayer: Lord, you teach us that harsh words stir up anger; a soft answer turns away wrath. Remaining peaceful is the example you exemplify. Peace is a position of power. When I get angry or upset, help me to remember that remaining peaceful pleases you. Amen.

Scripture for further reading: 1 Kings 5:12; 1 Chronicles 12:17; Psalm 29:11; Psalm 85:8.

Letting Things Go

Control is an illusion. Yet, letting go is one of the hardest things to do. When you remember that all things happen for a reason, it is much easier to let go and not try to control everything and everybody. Letting go is a conscious decision to stand aside and let others manage their own lives. Letting go is the conscious decision to let God do what only He can do. "My flesh and my heart may fail, but God is the strength of my heart and my portion forever" (Psalm 73:26). Let God be in control and put Him on the throne of your life.

Prayer: Lord, as I begin each day, there is work to be done. Forgive me when I set out with my plans and ask you to bless them. Help me loosen that tight grip on the wheel of my life. May your will, not mine, be done. I ask that you take complete control of my life and guide my steps. In Jesus' name, I pray. Amen.

Scripture for further reading: Psalm 34:17; Psalm 85:10–13; 1 Peter 5:7; Proverbs 16:3.

_____

_____

_____

_____

_____

_____

_____

What Does It Mean to Believe in Jesus?

Believing in Jesus is more than going to church on Sunday and being baptized. It's not even about being a good person. Believing in Jesus is admitting that you are a sinner – yes, we all mess up. Believing in Jesus is knowing we need a Savior. Believing in Jesus is understanding that there is no way to earn God's approval by doing good things. We could never do enough good to warrant receiving the gift of salvation that Jesus paid the price for when He died on the cross — this is what it means to believe in Jesus. He forgave us and has commanded us to forgive others. "But if you do not forgive others their sins, your Father will not forgive your sins" (Matthew 6:15).

Prayer: Lord Father, I admit that I am a sinner. I believe you died for me. I am forgiven, and salvation is my gift. You are the answer to victory in my struggles. Help me to forgive others as you have forgiven me. All my sin stems in pride. Lord, I need help with this. Father God, I ask you to change my heart to forgive others as I am forgiven. Come into my life now, Lord Jesus. I accept you as my Savior. Amen.

Scripture for further reading: Galatians 3:19–22; Philippians 2:9–11; Colossians 1:11–14.

_____

_____

_____

_____

_____

Easier Said Than Done

Trusting God is much easier said than done. It is a process that begins with giving God a try. As God blesses us, faith grows. As faith grows, challenges come, and faith is tested. When we cry out to God for mercy, He blesses us for trusting in Him. If faith were never tested, we would take it for granted and forget about God's goodness. Proverbs 3:5–8 encourages us to "Trust in the Lord with all your heart and lean not on your understanding; in all your ways submit to Him, and He will make your paths straight."

Prayer: Lord, during trials, forgive me when I try to fix things on my own. Forgive me when I reach for help from others before I reach out to you. I can't trust myself as I can trust you. I can't trust others as I can trust you. I experienced enough trials to know that nothing will get resolved until I reach out to my Creator first. May I honor you by walking through life, putting my faith and trust in you. Let the fire of faith burn in my heart. Amen.

Scripture for further reading: Job 4:17–19; Psalm 25:1–5; Psalm 40:3–5; Romans 4:5–8.

_____

_____

_____

_____

_____

_____

_____

Grace

What is your redeeming quality? Do you do good things, go to church, and serve in the community? Wonderful. But that will not get you into heaven. Nor are you condemned when you mess up. Nothing you do — good or bad — will earn you salvation or prevent you from it. Be redeemed by accepting the grace of Jesus Christ. Once you are one in spirit with Him, His love will melt your heart. You will know deep within your soul, that while you were once condemned, you are now saved. John 10:10 says, "The thief comes only to steal and kill and destroy; I have come that they may have life, and have it to the full."

Prayer: Father, thank you for your presence and grace. Your sacrifice on the cross saved me. It is because of your mercy and grace that I am one with you. You are my hope, forever. Amen.

Scripture for further reading: Acts 11:23–24; John 1:16–18; Romans 1:5–7; 11:5–6; 1 Corinthians 3:10–15.

_____

_____

_____

_____

_____

_____

_____

_____

Free From Guilt

Do you beat yourself up when you make a mistake? The devil enjoys watching you feel guilty about your shortcomings. You are the apple of Gods' eye. The creator of the universe breathed life into you. You are His masterpiece. With God, you're getting better every day, and He will help you through every challenge. First John 1:9 says, "If we confess our sins, He is faithful and just and will forgive us our sins and purify us from all unrighteousness." Guilt is a useless emotion. Learning from mistakes is essential for growth.

Prayer: Sovereign Lord, I think, say, and do things that don't make me happy. While others might define me by the foolish things I say or do, it's not who I am. I can learn from these mistakes and find a better way. Thank you for these learning opportunities. Thank you for changing me and teaching me the right ways. Thank you for loving me enough to make me more like Jesus. Amen.

Scripture for further reading: Colossians 2:16–19; Luke 15:3–7; Acts 3:19; 2 Peter 3:9.

_____

_____

_____

_____

_____

_____

Family and Friends

Family and friends are gifts from God. They are like stars — you don't always see them, but you know they're there. They encourage and enrich your life. They leave footprints on your heart. Time with friends and family becomes like a sanctuary of support from a stressful world. If we're not loving and kind to one another in this dark world, who else will be? First Timothy 5:8 reminds us, "Anyone who does not provide for their relatives, and especially for their household, has denied the faith and is worse than an unbeliever."

Prayer: Jesus, I thank you for family and friends. The enemy's goal is to separate us. God, when life takes us in different directions, help our bond remain, outlasting disagreements, changes, or separation. In your holy name, I pray. Amen.

Scripture for further reading: Ephesians 4:3–13; 2 Chronicles 30:12; Philippians 4:1–3.

Put First Things First

Busy people often let their relationships suffer — not intentionally, though. There just aren't enough hours in the day. Working hard is admiral, but it shouldn't be the top priority. How you spend your time and money indicates what your priorities are. God, family, and friends deserve more than your leftover time and attention. Putting first things first brings purpose, peace, and pleasure to life. Second Corinthians 1:12 reminds us, "Now this is our boast: Our conscience testifies that we have conducted ourselves in the world, and especially in our relations with you, with integrity and godly sincerity. We have done so, relying not on worldly wisdom but on God's grace."

Prayer: Father, relationships are just as meaningful as results. I often focus on one area over the other. Lead me to focus on what's most important. Put on my heart the people you want me to spend time with, listen to, love, and encourage. Put on my heart the results you want me to achieve and direct my steps. Thank you, Lord, for teaching me how to prioritize what's most important. Amen.

Scripture for further reading: Psalm 133:1–3; 1 Corinthians 12:12–26; John 17:20–26.

APRIL 24

Abide in Christ

Sadly, so many Christians don't understand what it means to abide in Christ. To abide in Him means spending time in His presence. It is getting away from everything and everybody that will distract you. Meditate and wait on God. Cling to Him, be at peace with Him, and trust in Him. There is a fantastic exchange that takes place when you spend time in His presence. When you give your life to Christ, you present to Him, everything you are, and everything you're not. What Christ gives you in return, is His glorious righteousness. John 15:5 says, "I am the Vine; you are the branches. If you remain in me and I in you, you will bear much fruit; apart from me you can do nothing."

Prayer: Lord, may I remain ever in your presence. In you, I am a calm and restful soul. Help me to go with you throughout the day, celebrating every joy and sharing every sorrow. God, come to live in me through the Holy Spirit. Amen.

Scripture for further reading: 1 John 3:19–24; 1 Corinthians 12:27–31; Ephesians 1:9–14.

Put God First

The story of the apostle Paul demonstrates the confusion believers had during his time. That same confusion exists today. Galatians shunned Gentiles because they didn't practice the religious law of circumcision. Paul urged the Galatians to die to religious doctrine so that they would live for Christ. Churches today also profess should and should not rules to follow. These laws act to take the focus from Christ. Get free from the oppression of religious law so you can truly experience God's power. First Corinthians 2:4–5 says, "My message and my preaching were not with wise and persuasive words, but with a demonstration of the Spirit's power so that your faith might not rest on human wisdom, but on God's power."

Prayer: When I'm worried about what people think, more than what you think, Lord, I'm not putting you first in my life. May I never confuse religion with a relationship with you. Help me know you intimately. Help me keep your commands, your judgments, and your statutes. I praise you, Lord, for you are good. Amen.

Scripture for further reading: Deuteronomy 8:10–17; Philippians 3:8–10; Revelations 2:3–5.

_____

_____

_____

_____

_____

_____

Add Leeway to Your Life

How well do you manage your time? Proverbs 21:5 says, "The plans of the diligent lead to profit as surely as haste leads to poverty." One unplanned phone call or an accident on the road can leave you stretched for time and stressed for the rest of the day. Put margin in your day.

Prayer: Lord, help me to be a good steward of time. Time is a precious resource. I don't have any more or less time than anyone else. Help me to add leeway to my life and spend my time wisely. Amen.

Scripture for further reading: Ephesians 5:15–17; John 9:4; 1 Corinthians 14:40.

_____

_____

_____

_____

_____

_____

_____

_____

_____

_____

_____

Atonement

Atonement is an Old Testament word. It is found once in the New Testament to refer to the atoning death of Christ to reconcile us with God. Atonement means to make amends. The devil tries to convince us to make a sacrifice, make amends, or accept punishment for our misdeeds. That is a lie. Romans 8:1–2 reveals, "Therefore, there is now no condemnation for those who are in Christ Jesus because through Christ Jesus the law of the Spirit who gives life has set you free from the law of sin and death." The law was powerless to do what only God could do by sending God's own Son. Because of His willing sacrifice, there is hope instead of condemnation.

Prayer: Lord, let me start this day with a clean slate. There is nothing I can do to cover my sins because you've already done that for me. Forgive me for my sins and change my ways. Thank you for atoning for my sins. Amen.

Scripture for further reading: 1 John 2:2; Isaiah 53:5–6; 2 Corinthians 5:21; Revelations 5:9.

_____

_____

_____

_____

_____

_____

_____

Impose

A teacher can't impose education on a student. A student must want to learn. Likewise, God chooses to persuade rather than impose himself on us. We need to follow His example. God does not make us love Him, nor does He make us do what's right. Similarly, we shouldn't impose our wants, wishes, and needs on others. We will never be perfect, but we can improve our thoughtfulness toward others. "For those who are led by the Spirit of God are the children of God" (Romans 8:14). The repentant sinner is a changed person and led by the Spirit, to be more like Jesus.

Prayer: Lord, I don't want to impose myself on others. When I'm stretched thin, or in trouble, I'm not very thoughtful. At those times, I impose on others to help me. Instead, may I recognize that you are my source and follow your excellent example of thoughtfulness. Show me a more excellent way. Amen.

Scripture for further reading: Romans 14:1–23; 2 Chronicles 7:14; Philippians 1:27.

_____

_____

_____

_____

_____

_____

_____

Stand Up

Peer pressure exists wherever there are people. People fiercely desire to be accepted — to be with others who share the same thoughts, interests, and circumstances. But when it comes to making decisions, you must stand up for what you believe is right. If you don't, you're standing for what is wrong. First Peter 1:13–21 says, "Therefore, with minds that are alert and fully sober, set your hope on the grace to be brought to you when Jesus Christ is revealed at His coming. As obedient children, do not conform to the evil desires you had when you lived in ignorance. But just as He who called you is holy, so be holy in all you do." Don't compromise with what you know to be right.

Prayer: Be with me now, Lord Jesus. Fill me with your holy presence. Thank you for your grace against adversity. Thank you for helping me stand against peer pressure, and all that is ungodly. Amen.

Scripture for further reading: Exodus 14:13–14; Psalm 33:11–15; Matthew 24:12–14.

_____

_____

_____

_____

_____

_____

_____

Finish the Race

Give it your all, whatever the task. Relying solely on human strength, abilities, and enthusiasm will only take you so far. Depend on the power of the Holy Spirit, be pure in heart, and expect miracles. With God, go after the goal with all your heart. You will see the great things that God can and will do to bless your efforts. Second Timothy 4:7–8 says, "I have fought a good fight, I have finished the race; I have kept the faith. Now there is in store for me the crown of righteousness, which the Lord, the righteous Judge, will award to me on that day — and not only to me, but also to all who have longed for His appearing."

Prayer: Lord, I ask for blessings of strength, encouragement, and conviction to complete the tasks ahead. I lean on the grace and power of the Holy Spirit to achieve all that is before me. I pray this in your name. Amen.

Scripture for further reading: Ephesians 2:10; Proverbs 19:20; Judges 2:7.

_____

_____

_____

_____

_____

_____

_____

_____

Positive Words

What you think affects your life, emotions, and attitudes. What you say has even more significance. Words are incredibly powerful — they are thoughts spoken and made eternal. Words of kindness and words of condemnation are returned in kind, and with greater intensity. Successful people control their words rather than letting their words control them. Use positive words to build relationships and create opportunities. Second Chronicles 10:7 says, "If you will be kind to these people and please them and give them a favorable answer, they will always be your servants." Two things matter in our daily lives, and that is results and relationships. Words are instruments that bring about positive or negative results and relationships. Be careful to examine what you think before you speak.

Prayer: God, help me work out any imperfections in my thoughts and speech. Amen.

Scripture for further reading: Psalm 19:14; Luke 4:33–37; 1 Peter 4:11; 1 Corinthians 2:6–10.

The Difference Between Success and Failure

When it comes to making mistakes, there are three kinds of people: those who are foolish, those who are successful, and those who become experts. A fool makes excuses for mistakes, while successful people gain experience from them, and experts are not frightened by their failings. "Then they cried out to the Lord in their trouble, and He brought them out of their distress" (Psalm 107:28). Failure is not an option: it exists when someone withdraws, blames, or makes excuses. Learn from your mistakes and ask God to help you find another way, find better resources, and give you the stamina to keep plowing forward.

Prayer: Lord, it's hard to make mistakes. It's less painful to learn from others' examples, reading the Bible, and listening to good advice, but sometimes we must learn the hard way — by making mistakes. Help me to look at these times as opportunities to grow. I cry out to you in my distress. Help me recognize the lesson to be learned and find the answer. Amen.

Scripture for further reading: Numbers 15:28–29; 2 Peter 3:17–18; Psalm 19:12–13; James 5:19.

_____

_____

_____

_____

_____

_____

Who Is as Perfect as You?

No matter how good a person is, at some point, they will disappoint you. Chances are, it's not intentional. It takes a long time to become a person of character. The truth is, none of us arrive in this world perfect. People change. People are perfected from glory to glory, from challenge to challenge, and from victory to victory. Just because someone doesn't treat you the way you want them to, doesn't mean they're not doing the very best they can. You must understand that and forgive them. No one is perfect, except our Lord. Follow Jesus' example when people disappointed Him. Pray for those who are less than ideal, forgive them, and leave them with loving words. "But if you do not forgive others their sins, your Father will not forgive your sins" (Matthew 6:15).

Prayer: Father, help me believe the best of everyone and know that you are not finished with them yet. Amen.

Scripture for further reading: 1 Corinthians 13:7; 1 Timothy 4:10; Ephesians 1:18–19.

_____

_____

_____

_____

_____

_____

_____

Accept It for What It Is

When someone hurts you, forgive them — not for their sake, but yours. Don't accept what happened, as acceptable. Acceptance doesn't mean it was fair. Acceptance means you take responsibility for repairing the pain that's inside you. Forgiveness lessens the pain. Do you want to be right, or do you want to be whole? Let go of the grudge. That's all. Forgiveness is hard, but it's the only answer. It helps to consider what the other person was going through. It helps to accept what happened without blame. It helps to face up to your part in the conflict. It helps to think of what you learned through the process. Then move forward happy and whole. "Teach me knowledge and good judgment, for I trust your commands" (Psalm 119:66).

Prayer: Lord, it is not natural for me to forgive someone who has hurt me, but that's what you want. Help me forgive so that it doesn't fester inside like a poison. You gave me a spirit of strength and power. You gave me a desire for joy and happiness. Forgive me for allowing others to hurt me. Forgive me for continuing to allow them to hurt me by not letting go of the pain. Help me to recognize and protect the life you created in me for your good pleasure. Help me move forward, happy, and whole. Amen.

Scripture for further reading: Galatians 5:13–14; Colossians 3:13; Luke 17:3–4; Mark 11:25.

_____

_____

_____

_____

_____

What Is Wrong With This Relationship?

Paul said, "Brothers and sisters, if someone is caught in a sin, you who live by the Spirit should restore that person gently. But watch yourselves, or you also may be tempted" (Galatians 6:1). While you should encourage others not to sin, you are to protect yourself from any sinful nature from associating with them. Get out of the relationship if it's detrimental. Judging the person by the world's criteria is different from making a judgment call about whether the relationship is a healthy one.

Prayer: God, help me to either restore healthy relationships or remove myself from unhealthy ones. Realizing a bond is unhealthy for me is not the same thing as judging the person. Thank you for helping me to distinguish the difference. Amen.

Scripture for further reading: Matthew 7:1–6; Hebrews 10:24–25; Proverbs 22:24–25; 2 Corinthians 15:33.

_____

_____

_____

_____

_____

_____

_____

The Spark That Ignites

Self-confidence is not the same as self-importance. The difference between the two is pride. Pompous people who flaunt their accomplishments, abilities, and affluence indulge in their self-importance. There's no room for humility in self-importance. Prideful self-importance burns bridges and destroys friendships. Self-confidence, on the other hand, makes room for humility. Humility doesn't mean that you think less of yourself — it means that you think of yourself less. It allows you to use accomplishments, abilities, and affluence to make a difference in the world. Self-confidence is the assurance that propels you forward to fulfill your heart's desire. Confidence is the spark that ignites greatness within you. First Peter 5:5 says, "In the same way, you who are younger, submit yourselves to your elders. All of you, clothe yourselves with humility toward one another, because God opposes the proud but shows favor to the humble."

Prayer: Lord, help me to be confident enough to make a difference, but make a difference with humility. Amen.

Scripture for further reading: Hebrews 4:16; Isaiah 32:17–18; Philippians 1:6; Philippians 3:3–5.

_____

_____

_____

_____

_____

_____

You Can't Change People

You will always find insecure, irritating, selfish, and rude people. If you walk away from them, you'll run into someone else just like them. So what are your options?

- Acknowledge that you are powerless to change them, and lift them in prayer.
- Be supportive and encouraging without being judgmental.
- Spend your time and energy improving your own life, instead of worrying about theirs.

Romans 2:4 asks us, "Or do you show contempt for the riches of his kindness, forbearance, and patience, not realizing that God's kindness is intended to lead you to repentance?" Ask God to provide you with understanding and the appropriate response.

Prayer: Lord, when people misbehave, let me respond in a manner acceptable to you. Help me, Lord, with kindness, forbearance, and patience. I pray that you bring about the change required in me to know when to support others, and when to focus on my affairs. There are boundaries on when the night ends, and morning begins. So, too, there should be boundaries on when to start and stop doing for others. What freedom in this knowledge. Thank you, Lord Jesus. Amen.

Scripture for further reading: Proverbs 19:20; Proverbs 13:20; 1 Corinthians 6:11; 2 Corinthians 4:16–18.

_____

_____

_____

I Ran Into a Stranger (paraphrased) Author Unknown

I ran into a stranger as he passed by, "Excuse me, please," I replied. Oh, so nice, this stranger and I — We were so polite to say good-bye.

But at home, a different story is told; How we treat our loved ones, young and old. Later that day, I cooked a meal; my daughter was beside me, standing still. When I turned, I nearly knocked her down. "Move," I said with a frown. She walked away; her little heart broken; I didn't realize how harshly I'd spoken. While I lay awake in bed, God's voice to me said, "While dealing with a stranger, common courtesy you use, but the children you love, you seem so rude. In the kitchen are flowers she picked for you; pink and blue. She stood quietly not to spoil the surprise, with the tears in her eyes." I rose from my bed and went to kneel by her bed: "Wake up, little girl, wake up." I said. "Are these flowers for me?" She smiled, "I found 'em, by the tree." "Daughter, I'm sorry for today." She said, "Oh, Mom, I love you, anyway."

Prayer: Lord, you love me more than the moon and the stars. Show me how to love those entrusted to my care, with the same depth, compassion, and tenderness that you give me. Romans 5:5 reminds me of the wisdom of your love: "And hope does not put us to shame, because God's love has been poured out into our hearts through the Holy Spirit, who has been given to us." Amen.

Scripture for further reading: Colossians 3:12; 2 Peter 1:5-9; Proverbs 11:16-17.

Confidentiality

For someone to confide in you, they must believe that you are trustworthy and will keep your promise of confidentiality. That means you must act in a way that will inspire them to believe in you — with small things and big things. They must feel that their secret is safe with you. You can help them deal with their problem, but you must not gossip to others about it. God hates gossip. "A gossip betrays a confidence, but a trustworthy person keeps a secret" (Proverbs 11:13).

Prayer: Lord, I pray that I inspire trust in others by keeping their affairs confidential, helping them, and encouraging them. Thank you for teaching me this lesson. May I instill this confidence in others. Reveal your Word in me. Amen.

Scripture for further reading: Proverbs 20:19; Matthew 12:36–37; Genesis 9:23.

Build Trust

The Bible reminds us to love one another. For love to flourish, there must be trust. Trust is the bedrock of a loving relationship. Love is the very essence of God and is the only eternal thing. "For where two or three gather in my name, there am I with them" (Matthew 18:20). God-centered friendships are created in love and built on trust. There are several ways to build trust.

T — Truly love one another
R — Respect one another
U— Understand one another
S — Share your true feelings
T — Take care of one another

Prayer: Lord, help me develop love and trust with my fellow brothers and sisters. I pray this in Jesus' name. Amen.

Scripture for further reading: 2 Corinthians 13:11–14; 3 John 1:1–8; 1 Thessalonians 1:2–10.

_____

_____

_____

_____

_____

_____

Confrontations

Disagreements occur in every relationship. A war of words rarely leaves you feeling vindicated. Worse yet, enraged relations are an appalling testimony to unbelievers. While Peter was ready to attack a group of angry men in the garden, Jesus's example, and calm demeanor, held him back. Proverbs 15:1–2 says, "A gentle answer turns away wrath, but a harsh word stirs up anger. The tongue of the wise adorns knowledge, but the mouth of the fool gushes folly."

Prayer: Lord, it takes spiritual maturity to walk away. It takes spiritual maturity to say the right things at the right time. I often nurse and rehearse an offense. Help me to respond appropriately. Be with me, Lord Jesus, during these difficult times, as my hope is in you. Amen.

Scripture for further reading: Romans 15:7; Acts 15:36–41; Acts 28:25–31.

God Blesses Those Who Work for Peace

Everyone experiences confrontation. Two people can never always agree on everything, all the time. Resolving conflict is an essential skill to develop, but it is hard work. People may not desire peace. Be assured of God's promise for those who pursue peace. Psalm 84:11 says, "For the Lord God is a sun and shield; the Lord bestows favor and honor; no good thing does He withhold from those whose walk is blameless." The Lord will give you His grace and glory when you do your part to keep the peace. God won't hold back any good thing from those who walk uprightly. To remain in peace is to remain in power.

Prayer: Lord, I know that you bless those who pursue peace. As surely as the morning follows the night, fortunate times follow difficult times. Help me keep peace and seek you through all times. Help me trust you more and find a better way to manage conflict. Amen.

Scripture for further reading: Numbers 25:10–13; Isaiah 26:3–4; Psalm 34:14–15; 120:6–7; Proverbs 16:7.

_____

_____

_____

_____

_____

_____

We Create Our Happiness

Deciding to discover and develop the love and goodness that exists within our souls brings true happiness. True happiness doesn't come from gaining physical or mental pleasure. In fact, the opposite is true: A lot of our unhappiness is derived from craving physical or mental pleasure. James 3:14–16 says, "But if you harbor bitter envy and selfish ambition in your hearts, do not boast about it or deny the truth. Such 'wisdom' does not come down from heaven but is earthly, unspiritual, demonic. For where you have envy and selfish ambition, there you find disorder and every evil practice."

Prayer: Lord, open my eyes to see what great things are in store for me. Forgive my grumblings. I choose to be thankful and happy for all that you provide. Help me look inside for all the love and goodness that is there. Help me to cherish these gifts and help them flourish in the beauty of life. I praise you for your goodness. Amen.

Scripture for further reading: James 3:17–18, James 5:13; 1 Corinthians 2:13–16; Deuteronomy 16:13–15.

Pray for Guidance

Are you confused about which way to turn? The Bible is the best source for guidance and direction. It is the most exceptional love letter ever written by the most celebrated author of all time. That author refers to Himself as our shepherd. A shepherd leads sheep to provision and protection. When you hear His Word, listen. John 10:14 says, "I am the good shepherd; I know my sheep and my sheep know me." He will guide you.

Prayer: Lord, help me to listen for your voice. Trusting only in you draws good to me and excellence from me. There is no greater prosperity than that of receiving the richness of your abundant blessings. Thank you, Lord Jesus. Amen.

Scripture for further reading: John 10:11–18; 1 Peter 2:25; Psalm 16:11; Psalm 19:7–14; Psalm; Mark 6:34.

_____

_____

_____

_____

_____

_____

_____

_____

_____

Vent Vertically

God's never surprised by your emotions. Negative emotions come from unmet needs. No one can meet these needs better than God. So, vent. But take your cares to God. Psalm 72:12 says, "For He will deliver the needy who cry out, the afflicted who have no one to help." During a time of need, try these two strategies:

- Make time for God your top priority.
- Find a quiet place where there are no distractions and invite Him in. It is refreshing for your soul.

Prayer: Lord, when I'm in despair, let me present my requests so that I may see your magnificence made manifest. You are my source, my comfort, and my strength. You are the answer in time of need. Amen.

Scripture for further reading: 1 Peter 3:12; Mark 11:24; John 15:14–15; Psalm 66:19.

_____

_____

_____

_____

_____

_____

_____

_____

Do You Want to Be Blessed, or Not?

We should strive for character confident enough to reject offense, and principled enough from inflicting it. In conflict, time heals nothing; it causes hurts to fester. Unresolved conflict is nothing more than sin; it blocks our fellowship with God and keeps our prayers from being answered. Love is the one word that encapsulates the Christian experience. Love overcomes offense. Proverbs 19:11 tells us, "A person's wisdom yields patience; it is to one's glory to overlook an offense."

Prayer: Lord, help me to love others as you love them. I don't want to block my fellowship with you or the blessings that come with having an intimate relationship with you. Yet I know that you can't abide where there is sin. Help me overlook an offense, show wisdom, and demonstrate patience so that I don't block the flow of your blessing in my life. Amen.

Scripture for further reading: Hebrews 12:1–5; Proverbs 28:9; Isaiah 59:2; Acts 7:26; Psalm 66:18.

_____

_____

_____

_____

_____

_____

Don't Fight Your Feelings

We are spiritual beings, having a human experience. We experience different emotions because of diverse worldly circumstances. Don't deny your feelings; they are gifts from God. But learn to control your feelings, so they don't control you. If you feel angry, emotions may provoke you to say or do something you'll be sorry for later. That's a sin. Many times, feelings are not so much about injustice as they are a warning that you need to take control of your life and set better boundaries. Don't get mad at others; instead, make a change to guard your heart, protect your time, or take better care of yourself. Recognize what actions your emotions are telling you. First Corinthians 8:1 says, "Those who think they know something do not yet know as they ought to know."

Prayer: God, if I give into my feelings of anger because a person offends me or doesn't live up to my expectations, forgive me. Keep me from saying or doing wrong things as a result. Instead, let me realize these feelings for what they are. I pray that you will help me gather my senses and understand the boundaries I should set to protect this treasure of life you created in me. Thank you for this gift of understanding. Amen.

Scripture for further reading: Jeremiah 17:9; Proverbs 28:26; Proverbs 14:12–13; Philippians 1:9–11.

Show Them You Care

People don't care how much you know until they know how much you care. This quote is attributed to President Theodore Roosevelt, John Maxwell, and many others. We can all relate to the truth of this saying. How can we show others we care about them? Primarily, we can listen, really listen to others. It tells them we value their opinion. Don't be like the people described in 2 Kings 17:14, which says, "But they would not listen and were as stiff-necked as their ancestors, who did not trust in the Lord their God." Listening is like giving others a precious gem. It is a treasure of great value.

Prayer: Lord, it's so comfortable to come up with all the answers. To help others, I offer solutions to problems I don't fully understand. Instead of allowing others to share their experience and finding their solutions, I jump to conclusions based on my experience, which may be very different from their experience. How selfish. I pray, Lord, that I will talk less. With your help, I pray to listen more. Help me to extend love and thoughtfulness by hearing what others think and feel. In Jesus' name, I pray. Amen.

Scripture for further reading: James 1:19; Proverbs 6:20; Titus 3:2; Proverbs 19:20; Matthew 7:2.

_____

_____

_____

_____

_____

Family

Family is one of the greatest gifts in life. But family is all too often taken for granted. The love that binds a family is a compelling thing. The family encourages us to be the best we can be despite seeing our worst. Family is the foundation of society. Family provides love and a sense of belonging. The letters in the word family stand for Father And Mother I Love You. The 7th beatitude tells us to cooperate instead of fight with them. Learn this, and find your place in God's family.

Prayer: Lord, bless my family. Help us forgive one another. May we be helpful and encouraging. Amen.

Scripture for further reading: Luke 8:19–21; Psalm 127:3–5; Colossians 3:21; Mark 10:9; Proverbs 17:6.

_____

_____

_____

_____

_____

_____

_____

_____

_____

Agree to Disagree

It is unrealistic to think that everyone will agree about everything all the time. God requires unity, not uniformity. If there is conflict, agree to disagree. Disagree without being disagreeable. Search for a solution. Ask God for answers. Fight the good fight of faith to find common ground. Pursue peace. When you've resolved to reunite and focus on friendship, the problem becomes less critical and loses relevance. "Submit to God and be at peace with Him; in this way prosperity will come to you" (Job 22:21).

Prayer: Lord, teach me to walk arm in arm with others, even if we don't see eye to eye. When possible, help us to get through thick and thin. It's not the worlds' way, but it's your way — it's a better way. Amen.

Scripture for further reading: Ecclesiastes 4:9–10; Colossians 3:12–14; Proverbs 24:5; Proverbs 27:5–6.

_____

_____

_____

_____

_____

_____

_____

_____

_____

Don't Give the Devil Permission to Disrupt

Disagreements are disruptive. Disagreements consume time and energy and take attention away from what is essential. The enemy is always trying to trigger situations to get you off-track and steal your joy. Don't be an easy target. Whatever the problem, the first thing to do is something. Attack the problem, but not the person. You can't find a solution consumed with finding blame. Proverbs 15:1 reminds us that, "A gentle answer turns away wrath, but a harsh word stirs up anger." Side-step the negative.

Prayer: Lord, during disagreements, I pray for reconciliation, if possible. When I focus on the problem, it's like putting a pebble close to my eye; it looks larger and blocks my vision. When I throw the pebble down, where it belongs, I put it in its right perspective. Open my eyes to see what the enemy is trying to do. Help me stay focused on what matters. Keep me in peace and joy. Help me sidestep the negative. In Jesus' name, I pray. Amen.

Scripture for further reading: Ephesians 6:12; 1 Corinthians 10:13; Hebrews 4:16; Isaiah 41:10.

Who Will Get Hurt?

A grudge is a strange thing. It usually only hurts the person who holds onto it. People who harbor a grudge are bitter and resentful. They want others to know they suffered. They want sympathy and support. They want revenge. The person the hatred is directed against, may or may not be guilty of an offense. People are not perfect. Chances are, no one intended to hurt or disappoint. Escape the prison of hostility and learn to forgive. "Bear with each other and forgive one another if any of you has a grievance against someone. Forgive as the Lord forgave you" (Colossians 3:13). A better option would be to give them the benefit of the doubt and forgive them.

Prayer: Lord, thank you for reminding me that harboring resentment toward others only hurts me. Remove my arrogance of holding a grudge and replace it with a changed heart of humility. Others are not perfect, nor am I. I pray that I do not offend anyone because of my imperfection. In Jesus' name, I pray. Amen.

Scripture for further reading: Psalm 30:5; Psalm 55:22; Romans 8:28; Philippians 4:6–7; Mathew 6:6.

_____

_____

_____

_____

_____

_____

Beware of False Teaching

False teachers are everywhere, trying to seduce you away from the true Word of God. Many who call themselves Christians are wolves among sheep, introducing new and false doctrine. "I warn everyone who hears the words of prophecy of this [Bible], which states, 'If anyone adds anything to them, God will add to that person the plagues described in this [Bible]. And if anyone takes words away from this [Bible] of prophecy, God will take away from that person any share in the tree of life and the Holy City'" (Revelations 22:18 –19). God is the beginning and end. He is three in one: The Father, Son, and Holy Spirit. Jesus is God for all eternity, and He will come again. Salvation comes from faith in Jesus. The word of God is God-breathed, accurate, and complete.

Prayer: Lord, I pray for all nations to return to follow Christ Jesus. I pray for all generations to know that Jesus Himself is the Word incarnate. I pray for every tongue around the world to confess that you are God. Amen.

Scripture for further reading: Ezekiel 13:9; Acts 20:28–30; Matthew 24:24; Matthew 16:11–12; 2 Timothy 4:3–4.

_____

_____

_____

_____

_____

_____

Where Do I Start?

Are you a person who takes the initiative? Do you anticipate what needs to be done and make it happen? When you show initiative, people notice. When you take the initiative, you gather momentum to get the job done. When you act, you gain the upper hand to execute your vision. "For Titus not only welcomed our appeal, but he is coming to you with much enthusiasm and on his initiative" (2 Corinthians 8:17).

Prayer: Lord, I want to take the initiative, but I don't want to insist on doing things my way. Let me seek your wisdom first and then take the lead, knowing that it will be the right decision. I ask for your guidance and trust that you'll lead me to find the resources to complete the task ahead. Amen.

Scripture for further reading: James 1:22; James 4:17; Matthew 7:21–24; Ezra 10:4; 1 Peter 1:13.

What's More Powerful Than Persistence?

When I was a child, I cried for hours when I lost the watch my Grandma gave me. I searched everywhere. I was miserable and made everyone around me miserable. After hours of distress, I finally came to the end of myself. I remembered Grandma taught me to pray with faith, so I cried out to God. I prayed, "God, you said that if I seek you, ask you to help me, and believe with all my heart, you will answer my prayer. I trust that you will hear me, God, and help me find my Grandmother's watch." When I finished my prayer, I reached down in the school cafeteria trash can, picked up a lunch bag, and looked inside to find that precious treasure. Yes, my Grandmother's watch was in the first bag I picked up after finishing my prayer of faith. I will always cherish and never forget my first spiritual experience. The humorous circumstance, is even more precious, as I reflect on God's sense of humor. Jeremiah 7:24 says, "But they did not listen or pay attention; instead, they followed the stubborn inclinations of their evil hearts. They went backward and not forward." Focus and persistence are powerful. Include God in the equation and experience His glory. Prayer opens the door for God to bring about supernatural results. Prayer makes God the focus to bring about extraordinary results.

Prayer: Lord, I come before your throne of grace and thank you for being a mighty God, full of power for the weak in spirit, and mercy for the downcast. Be with me Lord in every hour of every day. Amen.

Scripture for further reading: Colossians 1:11–12; Galatians 6:9; James 1:12; Ephesians 6:11.

Moral Courage

Moral courage maximizes life. Morality requires courage to think things through, stand up for what is right, and stay vigilant. The Bible teaches moral courage. Cowards, on the other hand, give up, cave in, and find the easy way. Acts 27:22 says, "But now I urge you to keep up your courage because not one of you will be lost." Take courage and know that God is with you. When you do, you will receive the victors' crown.

Prayer: Lord, give me the courage to live each day to stand up for what is right. In this wisdom, I find exceeding joy and fulfillment. Amen.

Scripture for further reading: Hebrews 6:11; Luke 2:19; 1 Corinthians 15:58; Deuteronomy 31:6–8.

_____

_____

_____

_____

_____

_____

_____

_____

_____

_____

Something to Celebrate

Confidence is the ability to feel that everything will be all right, even when circumstances are not. It's easy to feel confident when life is great. But are you sure of yourself when criticized, or when life is challenging? Do you know anyone with plenty of confidence but lacks faith in God? On the other hand, there are people with faith in God but none in themselves. God asks us to have both. Second Corinthians 3:4–5 states, "Such confidence we have through Christ before God. Not that we are competent in ourselves to claim anything for ourselves, but our competence comes from God." Nothing is impossible with God. That's something to celebrate!

Prayer: Lord, without you, I can do nothing. With you, I can do all things. In this confidence, I am excited about the infinite possibilities before me. Amen.

Scripture for further reading: Ephesians 6:10; Isaiah 41:10–13; 1 Corinthians 16:13; Psalm 23:1–4.

_____

_____

_____

_____

_____

_____

_____

My First Priority

What are the God-given gifts that allow you to accomplish amazing things? Be thankful for them, and celebrate them. There are some things you are not as gifted to perform. When you are weak, acknowledge God and make Him your priority. If you do, God promises to help you do even greater things. Acknowledging God in our weakness is also a cause for celebration. Give credit where credit is due. In all things, give God the glory. Philippians 4:13 says, "I can do all things, through [Christ] who gives me strength."

Prayer: Lord, I am an expression of your spirit. In this confidence, I know there is unlimited potential for me. Thank you, Lord, that as your child, I can accomplish far more than I could ever hope or imagine. Amen.

Scripture for further reading: Philippians 4:6; 1 Corinthians 2:4–5; 2 Corinthians 3:18; Psalm 8:3–9.

_____

_____

_____

_____

_____

_____

_____

_____

A Hospital for Sinners

The church is not a place for saints, but a hospital for sinners. It is a place to reflect on Jesus' love, words, and deeds. When you find a church home, it is a place to rest, and bring glory to God. Matthew 16:18 says, "And I tell you that you are Peter, and on this rock, I will build my church, and the gates of Hades will not overcome it." The church is a light to the world to find hope, peace, and truth.

Prayer: Lord, your church is my sanctuary. I pray your church reaches worshippers in all communities in the world. I pray for movements of worshippers to erupt, bringing honor and glory to your holy name. Stir the hearts of people to know you personally. Come into our hearts and fully reveal the splendor of your presence. Amen.

Scripture for further reading: Hebrews 10:24–25; Matthew 18:20; Matthew 28:19–20; 2 Timothy 2:24–26.

_____

_____

_____

_____

_____

_____

_____

_____

There Is No Other Way

Being Christian is not an ethical decision or a moral inspiration. Being Christian is an encounter with the Holy Spirit. Growing up, you've probably seen the picture of Jesus knocking at the door. Everyone has a choice to open the door of their heart and let Him in, or to leave it closed and reject Him. The only barrier to receive God's unspeakable love and salvation is freewill. Pray that all God's children will open the doors of their hearts to receive Him as their Savior, just as Joshua resolved in verse 24:15, which says, "But if serving the Lord seems undesirable to you, then choose for yourselves this day whom you will serve....But as for me and my house, we will serve the Lord." There is no other way.

Prayer: Lord, I know that you love me as far as the east is from the west, which has no end. The one who counts the most loves me. My heart is open to receive you, Lord, as my Savior. Amen.

Scripture for further reading: Joshua 24:15 John 3:6–8; Romans 8:2–6; 1 John 4:16.

_____

_____

_____

_____

_____

_____

_____

Let's Party

A hardened heart is a stubborn heart. It is a heart that has turned against God. There is no rest for those who have hardened their hearts. The Holy Spirit fills the heart of those who turn to Jesus. Don't resist God. Resist the Devil. "I will give you a new heart and put a new spirit in you; I will remove from you your heart of stone and give you a heart of flesh. And I will put my Spirit in you and move you to follow my decrees and be careful to keep my laws" (Ezekiel 36:26–27). Who in their right mind wouldn't want that? Pray to soften hearts everywhere and for all time. Pray for the world to receive the love and goodness of God. There is a grand celebration of angels rejoicing in heaven, each time a heart turns to God. Let's party!

Prayer: Lord, fill my heart, my life, and my future with the right desires and a new spirit. I pray that you will soften the hearts of those who don't know you. Living a life with you makes my heart sing and my soul rejoice. Living a life with you is a cause for celebration. Amen.

Scripture for further reading: Jeremiah 17:9; Jeremiah 31:3; Deuteronomy 7:9; Zephaniah 3:17; Romans 8:37–39.

_____

_____

_____

_____

_____

_____

_____

All Men Are of One Author

A novelist creates trials and tribulations throughout a manuscript. From chapter to chapter, the characters pull through and triumph over seemingly insurmountable challenges. Any great story has a setting, plot, character, conflict, and a resolution. A great story is precisely what the author of all life, God, has created for you. He shapes you, molds you, and more than anything else, He loves you. If the author of a novel can bring about a triumphant conclusion, how much more will your Father in Heaven do for you? That's a promise in Psalm 34:10, which says, "Those who seek the Lord lack no good thing."

Prayer: Lord, your power is profound. As the author of my life, you transform me through trials and tribulations, and in the end, will celebrate with me, the crowning conclusion in victory. You have overcome the world. I know full well that any challenge will result in the ultimate good. Thank you for creating the story of my life. Amen.

Scripture for further reading: John 14:6; Matthew 9:36–38; Luke 14:23; Romans 10:1.

_____

_____

_____

_____

_____

_____

An Increase in Your Bank Account

Relationships are like bank accounts. When you speak and act kindly, you are depositing into that relationship. If you talk and act rudely, you are making a withdrawal. As you'd like to increase the value of your bank account, you should increase the value of your relationships. The ability to develop stronger relationships is the key to success in your personal life and your career. First Thessalonians 4:11–12 offers additional guidance to increase the value of relationships with instructions to make it "your ambition to lead a quiet life: You should mind your own business and work with your hands... so that your daily life may win the respect of outsiders and so that you will not be dependent on anybody."

Prayer: Little children fight, scream, and bully, to get their way. It would be ridiculous for adults to act that way, yet we sometimes do. Thank you, Lord, for showing me a better way. Help me to make more deposits than withdrawals in my relationships. Amen.

Scripture for further reading: Matthew 5:14–16; Philippians 2:15; Colossians 4:4–6; 1 Peter 2:12.

Forget About It and Find Freedom

Concern is a natural and healthy emotion. But it is unhealthy when it turns into worry and anxiety. We can choose to live with the emotional and psychological damage of concern or live in the power of God's love. In a soccer game, you can think about the past ten failed goal attempts. Instead, take the shot, forget the past, and focus on the opportunity in front of you. The consequence of worry can cause you to lose confidence and miss the shot. The freedom to give it to God allows you to relax and take a second, third, or even fourth chance. First Corinthians 10:13 says, "No temptation has overtaken you except what is common to mankind. And God is faithful; He will not let you be tempted beyond what you can bear. But when you are tempted, He will also provide a way out so that you can endure it."

Prayer: Lord, what freedom in not having to be perfect. What freedom in focusing on you. Letting go of all that keeps me from taking a chance at the moment, is freedom. All power, honor, and glory to you. Amen.

Scripture for further reading: Job 26:7–14; Romans 1:20; Romans 15:13; Ephesians 3:20; 2 Peter 1:3.

Freedom From Bondage

It's no accident that you exist. You were born for a purpose. That purpose is to do something that will make the world a better place. "But I have raised you up for this very purpose, that I might show you my power and that my name might be proclaimed in all the earth" (Exodus 9:16). There is no higher purpose than to be like Christ, fellowship with Him, and inspire others to live with Him. In God, there is freedom. Ask yourself often, "Do people see Jesus in me?"

Prayer: Lord, many people are in some form of bondage: addictions, guilt, insecurity, and pride, to name a few. The list goes on. Life in you is freedom. As I fellowship with you, I am encouraged to be set free from anything that binds. Thank you, Lord, Jesus. Amen.

Scripture for further reading: Matthew 18:18; Romans 12:2; 2 Corinthians 3:17–18; 1 John 2:6.

_____

_____

_____

_____

_____

_____

_____

_____

155

Power in Prayer

Faith is the substance of things hoped for. The power of prayer increases as a person's faith increases. When a friend or family member is sick, hold on to faith powerful enough to believe for healing. James 5:14–16 says, "Is anyone among you sick? Let them call the elders of the church to pray over them and anoint them with oil in the name of the Lord. And the prayer offered in faith will make the sick person well; the Lord will raise them up....Confess your sins to each other and pray for each other so that you may be healed. The prayer of a righteous person is powerful and effective."

Prayer: Lord, you look all over the world to strengthen those whose hearts long for you. Please help those in my life whose minds are weary with fear, or their bodies are weak with sickness. Grant me the ever-present guidance of your Spirit to pray powerfully for those I love. Amen.

Scripture for further reading: Matthew 6:9–13; Matthew 21:22; John 14:13–14; Luke 18:1; Proverbs 15:29.

It's Possible

What joy a child's smile can bring to an aging grandparent. This little difference can make a big difference in the grandparent's demeanor, health, and purpose. One discovery in the cure for a disease can produce massive worldwide benefits. One small step to recycle can have long-lasting effects on our planet. God rewards every act of faith, even with the potential to impact the world substantially. Think about the influence of just one person, Martin Luther King, who simply stood up for what he believed. One man who acted with courage was responsible for changing government policy and impacting peoples' lives in a very significant and meaningful way. So, it is with you. You influence the world around you with your words and actions. Could it be, that your speaking one kind word at the right place and at the right time, could eventually unfold to bring peace in another part of the world? It's possible. "Go home in peace. I have heard your words and granted your request" (1 Samuel 25:35).

Prayer: Father, because of your grace, I can make a significant difference in the lives of those within my circle of influence. Then they impact other people's lives within their spheres of influence. And the ripple effect expands to include their circle of influence. Thinking about the possibilities from the connectedness of all lives, brings hope for a brighter day. I pray that everyone who reads this message realizes the difference their life can make. Amen.

Scripture for further reading: Psalm 32:11; Psalm 98:1–9; Psalm 117:1–2; Acts 15:3; Deuteronomy 6:6–7.

_____

_____

_____

How Do I Master This One?

There are enormous amounts of literary works about love. Love is a powerful force that is complicated by varied depths, emotions, and time. Love for a friend is not the same as love for fellow man. Love has many ups and downs. Love takes many forms and fashions. Sometimes love is affectionate, while other times, it appears in compassion. Love can be exhilarating, and it can be exhausting. Love is beautiful, but it's also hard work. Love is hard work, even with loveable people. It's hard enough to understand and express appreciation for friends and family, but God also instructs us to love our enemies. Romans 12:9–10 goes further, saying that "Love must be sincere…Be devoted to one another in love. Honor one another above yourselves."

Prayer: Lord, where do I start? Love is a tough concept to master. I need help. I especially will need insight on how to love my enemies. As I lean on you, I can start with baby steps: I can demonstrate kindness. I can find some small, tangible way to help others. I trust you to lead me through this process. Amen.

Scripture for further reading: 1 John 4:16; Proverbs 20:6–7; Song of Solomon 8:6; 1 Corinthians 13:1–13.

_____

_____

_____

_____

_____

_____

He Will Never Give up on You

Fear is brought about by a wrong thought or expected danger. Fear results in a host of negative physical and emotional symptoms. The best weapons against fear are prayer and trust in God's faithfulness. God is more powerful than anything or anyone that will come against you. God will never leave you or give up on you. Psalm 34:4 says, "I sought the Lord, and He answered me; He delivered me from all my fears." Repeat this verse every time you are afraid.

Prayer: Lord, with you, I feel like an eagle soaring, no matter how hard the wind blows. Despite circumstances, my life is brighter when I put my trust in you. Thank you for delivering me from my fears. Amen.

Scripture for further reading: Psalm 103:1–5; Exodus 19:3–6; 2 Thessalonians 3:3; Isaiah 41:10; Psalm 91.

_____

_____

_____

_____

_____

_____

_____

Prosperous and Successful

Success means different things to different people. Know what success means to you. Once you determine what you want to achieve, plan steps to accomplish the goal. Organize your thoughts by writing them down. Then develop a timeline and assign specific deadlines in your planner for the steps required. Go after your dream, step-by-step. Otherwise, you may never get around to accomplishing your goals, or you may be overwhelmed and never do anything. If you don't prioritize what's important, you'll be left dealing with whatever life throws at you. "Lord, God of my master Abraham, make me successful today" (Genesis 24:12).

Prayer: God, any appearance of lack is a misconception and does not define me. Prioritize my steps. Amen.

Scripture for further reading: Psalm 1:1–3; Proverbs 16:3; 1 Kings 2:3; Luke 16:10–11; Deuteronomy 8:18.

_____

_____

_____

_____

_____

_____

_____

_____

What to Do With Chaos

When the world comes at you, it is tempting to become angry, negative, or discouraged. Distractions can be frustrating, too. Technology, unexpected work issues, and surprise family visits can derail your schedule. And why does everything happen at once? Our enemy wants to do everything possible to prevent you from consulting with the one who will turn the chaos into order. Here's a thought: to restore tranquility, create a sanctuary, a place to pray, and spend quiet time in the presence of the Almighty. Push away any negative thoughts. Be rejuvenated. Know peace that comes from experiencing God's presence within. Serenity restores strength, confidence, and joy. "Restore to me the joy of your salvation and grant me a willing spirit, to sustain me" (Psalm 51:12).

Prayer: Holy Spirit, produce your fruit of love and joy in me (Galatians 5:22). Amen.

Scripture for further reading: Amos 9:14; Luke 10:38–42; James 4:7; Mark 6:31; Mark1:35.

Did I Step in Something, or Is That My Attitude That Stinks?

You are what you think. If you think negatively, you get negative results. If you nurse and rehearse negative thoughts, you will experience a negative environment. The same is true when you think positive thoughts; you get positive results. Most successful people possess one common characteristic, and that is that they focus on the positive. When tempted with a negative thought, fill your mind with hope, purpose, opportunity, and good. Your thoughts affect your attitude. Your attitude will either draw others to you or drive them away. Second Corinthians 5:17 reminds us, "Therefore, if anyone is in Christ, the new creation has come: The old has gone, the new is here."

Prayer: Lord, create in me a positive way of thinking, speaking, acting, and being. Mold me, shape me, and make me all that you want me to be. Amen.

Scripture for further reading: Ecclesiastes 3:1; Isaiah 40:31; Job 8:7; Isaiah 43:18–19; Philippians 3:13.

_____

_____

_____

_____

_____

Win the Day

I opened a fortune cookie that said, "Many a false step was made by standing still." God put the desire in every one of us to improve. There will be no progress if we refuse to step out in faith. Ephesians 2:10 makes it clear that God created us for more and states, "For we are God's handiwork, created in Christ Jesus to do good works, which God prepared in advance for us to do." Many postpone action out of fear. Sometimes fear shows its face under the guise of perfection or timing. One of the most powerful tools in the toolbox in conquering fear is to define it. Whatever is holding you back, slay that dragon. No matter how big the opponent, be determined to tackle it bravely. Next, clear your vision for what you want to accomplish. Commit to one goal. Don't pursue other options that will get you off track. Lastly, resolve to improve. Go to a higher level. Be so good that no one can ignore you. Focus on wins to stay motivated. Every day, name three wins, and three things that would make the day better. Your future is part chance, part choice. Winning is a choice.

Prayer: Lord, I declare that I will step out in faith, for it pleases you. Give me a clear vision. I will glorify you by committing to improve. Change me from the inside out. Do the work in me Lord, that transforms me on the inside and works its way out, to accomplish what you have prepared me to do. Finish your work in me. Amen.

Scripture for further reading: James 4:17; Colossians 3:2; 3:23–24; 1 Peter 1:13; Proverbs 6:6.

_____

_____

_____

_____

For Better Results, Shine a Light

Be a beacon of light. When you build others up in your mind, it causes you to like them. Not only that, but they will also like you in return. People tend to live up to the high opinion others have of them. The dynamics of this tendency often precedes an increase in self-esteem. What an opportunity to help improve the lives of others. It is devastating to witness a parent who berates a child's misconduct, knowing what it does to their self-esteem. A manager's admonishment of a subordinate for an honest mistake likewise extinguishes the fire of their spirit. Tearing others down serves no useful purpose and alienates one from the other. A more productive approach is to "Encourage one another and build each other up, just as in fact you are doing" (1 Thessalonians 5:11).

Prayer: Lord, you created everyone with exceptional ability and character. Everyone is precious in your sight and designed for an extraordinary purpose. Help me to recognize and inspire that uniqueness in them. Amen.

Scripture for further reading: Hebrews 10:24–25; Ephesians 2:10; 1 Corinthians 12:4–10; Isaiah 28:24–26.

_____

_____

_____

_____

_____

_____

Unlimited Possibilities

When you make up your mind about something and don't leave room for other options, you can dig yourself into a rut. When my husband and I were first married, he lost a lot of weight. It seemed to me that if his mother never prepared a kind of food for him growing up, he wouldn't try it. Some people have confidence only in the tried and true. He said he didn't like to eat lamb. Well, come to find out, he'd never eaten lamb. Because lamb wasn't familiar to him, he convinced himself that he wouldn't like it. One day I brought home gyros with a blend of beef and lamb. I'm sure he assumed it was 100% beef. Guess what. He loved it. His changed perspective about lamb could apply to other areas of life, too. If we want different results, we must be open to other possibilities, try new things, and get a new perspective. "Sing to him a new song; play skillfully, and shout for joy" (Psalm 33:3).

Prayer: Lord Jesus, help me leave room in life for the infinite opportunities and remarkable experiences available through you. You are the great creator. There are unlimited possibilities beyond the scope of my limited knowledge and understanding. May your joy be full in me. Amen.

Scripture for further reading: Isaiah 43:15; 2 Corinthians 4:16–18; Lamentations 3:21–23; Luke 2:40.

_____

_____

_____

_____

_____

Making a Big Difference

There are so many things you can do to make a significant impact in the world. Make people happy. Console the hurting. Cook for a shut-in. Reach out to a lonely friend. Volunteer at a shelter. Anything that prevents you from making this kind of contribution, get rid of it. Does anger prevent you from seeing others' needs? Does pride keep you from helping the less privileged? Are we too busy to help others? Whatever it is, ask God to help you get past it. It is written in 1 John 1:9, "If we confess our sins, He is faithful and just to forgive us our sins and purify us from all unrighteousness."

Prayer: Lord, help me to leave the world a better place than I found it. Amen.

Scripture for further reading: James 5:20; Matthew 25:40–41; Hebrews 13:16; Galatians 6:2; Luke 3:11.

Poise

Let's face it. Life happens. People with poise accept that a problem exists and take responsibility to find a solution. Do you respond to stress with anger, grudges, or despair? How do you push past pain? Here's a process that works:

- Identify the injury or insult. What happened? How did you feel?
- Identify what needs to happen. What do you need to hear? What do you wish had happened?
- Identify the benefit. What did you learn? Are you stronger? Did you respond like the kind of person you wish to be?

When you face what happened, you will learn to control your emotions instead of letting them control you. You will be better prepared to respond with poise. Gain knowledge and meet the challenge with dignity. Job 37:16 says, "Do you know how the clouds hang poised; those wonders of Him who has perfect knowledge?"

Prayer: Lord, help me respond with poise so that I may turn my most difficult times into my finest hour. Amen.

Scripture for further reading: Ecclesiastes 8:1–6; Colossians 4:6; Proverbs 16:10–20.

_____

_____

_____

_____

_____

Get Up

Everyone has failed at something. Successful people usually fail many times. A trait that helps define success is to get up one more time than you fall. Do you remember when you learned how to ride a bike? What happened if you stopped trying? What happened if you tried harder? Failure is the best teacher. Relax and reflect. Don't make excuses; don't find blame; don't get discouraged. Acknowledge your mistake; then failure can make you better. Learning from your mistakes allows you to get back up and try again. "Have I not commanded you? Be strong and courageous. Do not be afraid; do not be discouraged, for the Lord your God will be with you wherever you go" (Joshua 1:9).

Prayer: Lord, help me never give up and try, try, and try again. Give me the courage to get up and always try again. Amen.

Scripture for further reading: Jeremiah 8:4; Isaiah 43:18; Proverbs 24:16; Psalm 119:71; Psalm 145:14.

Conversation Skillset

Conversation skill is a gift shared by the most successful people. The ability to adequately express yourself in any situation gives you an image of poise, intelligence, and competence. Too often, people are focused on getting their perspective heard, hurrying to get the job done, or dominating the conversation. Self-centered conversations are unpleasant and ineffective. Colossians 4:6 tells us, "Let your conversation be always full of grace, seasoned with salt, so that you may know how to answer everyone."

Prayer: Lord, I pray that I may be more fully engaged in conversations. May my speech be gracious, my motives pure, and my heart sincere. Help me to listen more and be genuine and kind in my response. Help me express my ideas and opinions positively so that others are free to respond likewise. Amen.

Scripture for further reading: Ephesians 4:29; 1 Peter 2:9; 1 Thessalonians 5:18; Proverbs 10:32; Proverbs 16:24.

Real Success

Ordinary people are rarely persecuted. Successful people, on the other hand, are more subject to vicious and unfair treatment. Success brings persecution, jealousy, and envy. Be secure in living a life centered on God. God will reward you to the very end. "They will receive blessing from the Lord and vindication from God his Savior" (Psalm 24:5).

Prayer: Lord, the world teaches us to chase after power and position. But I know that real power and status come when we choose to serve you. Let me show kindness to those who are not kind. Let me show patience with those who are rude. Let me show forgiveness for those who don't ask for it. Let me show love to a hurting world. Amen.

Scripture for further reading: James 5:1–11; Colossians 3:15–17; 1 Corinthians 15:48–49.

_____

_____

_____

_____

_____

_____

_____

_____

_____

If I Just Had More Money

God's okay with your making money, but He doesn't want you to serve it. Those who serve money make their priority to seek success, careers, wealth, and power, none of which bring fulfillment. Those who seek a relationship with God know that He provides everything. The Bible says that we should be content because God will provide us with all our needs. "Whoever loves money never has money enough; whoever loves wealth is never satisfied with his income. This too is meaningless" (Ecclesiastes 5:10–11).

Prayer: Lord, I know that living in debt is living beyond my means. Not being satisfied with my income is a curse of my own making. Forgive me, Lord, and deliver me from this kind of oppression. May I be a good steward of the time and money you so graciously provide. Amen.

Scripture for further reading: Proverbs 13:11; Luke 3:14; 1 Timothy 6:10; 1 Timothy 6:17–19; Proverbs 3:17; Proverbs 10:4.

_____

_____

_____

_____

_____

_____

_____

_____

Only Way for Miraculous Blessing

Many people of faith fall short of experiencing God's glory. They limit the infinite abundance of God's favor and blessing by not practicing what they know to be true. Forgiving others is a requirement. We convince ourselves that we forgive others, yet we still harbor resentment towards them. Holding on to resentment is like swallowing poison and hoping someone else dies. Forgiving others doesn't accept what happened, as right, but letting go of the resentment serves to purify your heart and soul. Matthew 5:8 states, "Blessed are the pure in heart, for they will see God."

Prayer: Lord, the way to a pure heart is to forgive. I ask forgiveness for every impure thought, feeling, emotion, word, or action. As much as I can bear, reveal my iniquities so that I can account for them. I seek your gentle hand to guide me to a pure heart. If there is bitterness, anger, envy, jealousy, or any unclean thing in me, restore in me the innocence of a pure heart. In Jesus' name, I pray. Amen.

Scripture for further reading: Proverbs 22:19; 1 Timothy 1:5–7; Ephesians 5:3–10.

_____

_____

_____

_____

_____

You Can't Get Revenge

Revenge has no place in the life of a Christian. When someone has offended you, is your first inclination to take revenge? That's human nature. But God wants you to use this incident as an opportunity to learn something other than vengeance. It is an opportunity to solve the problem in a way that will honor God and offer benefits to everyone involved. Revenge begets revenge. No one wins; worse yet, there is no end to the hostility. There's a better way. Romans 12:17–18 says, "Do not repay anyone evil for evil. Be careful to do what is right in the eyes of everyone. If it is possible, as far as it depends on you, live at peace with everyone. Do not take revenge, my dear friends, but leave room for God's wrath."

Prayer: Lord, I accept what it says in the Bible, and ask you to help me in every situation, to find a better way. Amen.

Scripture for further reading: Exodus 14:14; Leviticus 19:18; Ezekiel 25:15–17; 2 Thessalonians 1:6.

The Shield of Faith Protects

Others don't make you mad; you allow yourself to get mad. Your choice when provoked is to either act on your emotions or be acted on by them. You can stay in control by remaining in faith. Try spelling faith like this:

Feel — Get in touch with how you feel. Are you embarrassed, angry, lonely, or abandoned?
Act — You can either withdraw, be aggressive, or find peace. Choose peace.
Improve — Would your behavior improve if your pastor was watching? Choose to stay in control.
Tell — The devil will put an idea in your head to make you mad. Tell yourself another story.
Hear — Hear and see what the facts are. Is there any evidence to support their side of the story, or yours?

Ephesians 6:16 says, "Take up the shield of faith, with which you can extinguish all the flaming arrows of the evil one."

Prayer: Father God, when I allow people to upset me, help me to stay in faith. Amen.

Scripture for further reading: Proverbs 16:32; Ephesians 3:14–20; Matthew 7:16–20.

_____

_____

_____

_____

His Way or My Way

There is a choice to make in every situation — my way or God's way. If I choose my way, God will leave me on my own. When I ask God to be part of every situation, He will guide me to do things His way. His ways are higher. Deuteronomy 30:16–17 says, "I command you today to love the Lord your God, to walk in obedience to Him, and to keep His commands, decrees, and laws; then you will live and increase, and the Lord your God will bless you.... But if your heart turns away and you are not obedient... you will certainly be destroyed."

Prayer: Lord, through your grace, I know what is right. I confess that I try to take control of situations, instead of letting go and letting you do what only you can do. I know your plans for me are outstanding. Help me cooperate with your plan for my life. Amen.

Scripture for further reading: Hebrews 13:20–21; Hebrews 10:36; Micah 6:8; 1 Peter 2:15; John 6:38–40.

_____

_____

_____

_____

_____

_____

_____

Power of Persuasion

First Corinthians 2:3–4 says, "I came to you in weakness and fear and trembling. My message and my preaching were not with wise and persuasive words, but with a demonstration of the Spirit's power so that your faith might not rest on human wisdom but on God's power." Paul's efforts to persuade would not be practical without two essential elements. To be persuasive, first begin in prayer, accessing the power of the Holy Spirit. Second, to be truly compelling, the content of the message must be grounded in truth. Present the facts, state your conclusion, and make it safe for others to express their views.

Prayer: Lord, I am more apt to listen when people are kind and gentle than when they are in my face and yelling. Lord, I pray that in every appeal, I seek you first and stay grounded in truth. I ask you to guide me in wisdom at these times to be persuasive and not abrasive. Amen.

Scripture for further reading: 2 Corinthians 6:4–13; Ephesians 6:19–20; Philippians 1:15–18.

_____

_____

_____

_____

_____

_____

_____

Love the Unlovable?

Are you convinced that there's someone in your life that not even their mother could love? Then pray like a maniac. Get on your knees and ask God to perform a miracle in them. Not for them: Do it for God. Second Thessalonians 2:13–14 reminds us, "But we ought always to thank God for you, brothers and sisters loved by the Lord, because God chose you as firstfruits to be saved through the sanctifying work of the Spirit and through belief in the truth. He called you to this through our gospel, that you might share in the glory of our Lord Jesus Christ." God desires that we make ourselves available to do His work, and through the gospel, make known the glory of the Lord.

Prayer: Lord, unlovable people teach me many things. I learn to love them, pray for them, or show them the light of your favor, goodness, righteousness, and truth. It is going to be a miracle to learn to love them. And with your help, Lord, I know that's just what I will do. Amen.

Scripture for further reading: Ephesians 5:8–17; Colossians 1:15–20; Philippians 2:5–8.

Worry

Worry is the dark place in the soul where negative emotions are developed. Worry produces anxiety, mental and physical illness, and fear. Worry has never fixed anything. We worry because we don't trust God. "Come to me, all you who are weary and burdened, and I will give you rest. Take my yoke upon you and learn from me, for I am gentle and humble in heart, and you will find rest for your souls" (Matthew 11:28–29).

Prayer: Lord, help me to trade worry with worship. Help me to exchange fear with faith. Remind me that I can count on you. Remind me that anxiety and sadness don't suit a sacred day. I give my cares to you. Amen.

Scripture for further reading: Luke 12:22–31; Luke 21:14–15; Matthew 6:25–34.

_____

_____

_____

_____

_____

_____

_____

_____

_____

_____

Freedom From Those Who Offend

When someone offends you, forgive them. Learn something about others that helps you find compassion for them. It's OK if you don't like them. It's OK if you don't want to spend time with them. But it's not OK to hold unforgiveness toward them. Your freedom from pain is in forgiveness. Unforgiveness is a sin. God will not function in your sin. Forgiveness allows God's abundant and glorious blessings to continue in your life. Psalm 119:32 says, "I run in the path of your commands, for you have broadened my understanding." Your understanding has set me free.

Prayer: Jesus, I pray that victims of serious crimes focus on what is eternal. Comfort those who are afflicted and show them how to respond in peace and love. There is freedom in forgiveness, freedom from the internal prison of anger, bitterness, and hatred that rages within and destroys the soul. Vindicate those who suffer, and bless them with the promises for those who forgive. Amen.

Scripture for further reading: Romans 6:15–18; Romans 8:1–4; Galatians 5:1.

Everlasting Implications

Jesus knew His fate. The last thing He told the disciples, was to, "Pray that you will not fall into temptation" (Luke 22:40). If you knew you were going to die, don't you think the last thing you'd tell your loved ones would be the most important? Temptation is anything that would keep us from doing God's will. The world is full of temptations. Jesus knew that we would need to access the extraordinary power of God to resist temptation. When temptation comes, consider the lasting significance of the choices you make. Pray that you will not fall into temptation.

Prayer: Lord, let these words of wisdom fall on my heart. I pray that I will not fall into temptation. Keep me from temptation. Amen.

Scripture for further reading: Colossians 3:5–10; Ephesians 6:10–12; Philippians 1:9–11.

_____

_____

_____

_____

_____

_____

_____

_____

_____

Love One Another

Jesus desires that we might know the extent of God's love. "I pray also for those who will believe in me through their message, that all of them may be one, Father, just as you are in me and I am in you. May they also be in us so that the world may believe that you have sent me. I have given them the glory that you gave me, that they may be one as we are one – I in them and you in me – so that they may be brought to complete unity. Then the world will know that you sent me and have loved them even as you have loved me" (John 17:20–23). The commandment to love God with all our heart, mind, and soul, and the command to love one another, are according to Jesus, the most important commandments. Strive to increase love for God and others. Wherever there is love, God is there also. God is perfect love.

Prayer: Lord, your commandment to love others is pure, yet challenging. My family consists of some in-laws and outlaws. Help me to love them alike. You are the king of perfect love. We are all justified by our faith expressed through love. I love you, Father. Amen.

Scripture for further reading: Galatians 5:2–6; Colossians 1:3–6; Philippians 2:1–4.

Rain or Shine

Victory is sweet. It lets you know what you can accomplish with the gifts and talents that God has given you. But failure is also sweet. Failure can be a source of information and wisdom. Failure can show you what wrong assumptions you've made or where your steps were off course. Cherish them both. First John 5:3–4 says, "[God's] commands are not burdensome, for everyone born of God overcomes the world."

Prayer: Lord, you are with me through rain or shine, and through ups and downs. There is cause to celebrate in every circumstance. My times are in your hands. While I pray for more blessings than trouble, I know that everything I experience is for the fulfillment of your good and glorious purpose. Amen.

Scripture for further reading: 2 Corinthians 6:1–10; Philippians 2:14–18; Colossians 2:9–10.

_____

_____

_____

_____

_____

_____

_____

_____

You've Got This

When times get tough, the tough get going. That's right. When trials come, immediate action is required. When challenges arise, don't give your confidence away. Stand your ground. Decide to persevere. When you do the will of God, you will receive your reward. It's never too late to do something. Put on the full armor of God and fight the good fight with faith, truth, righteousness, peace, and knowing that you are the apple of your Father's eye, who is above all things. Romans 8:37–39 says, "In all these things we are more than conquerors through Him who loved us. For I am convinced that neither death nor life, neither angels nor demons, neither the present nor the future, nor any powers, neither height nor depth, nor anything else in all creation, will be able to separate us from the love of God that is in Christ Jesus our Lord."

Prayer: Lord, thank you for the confidence I have because of your amazing love. What victory awaits as I move forward using all the tools available to fight and defeat every challenge I face. It is in this same confidence that your church can overcome all the evil that is in the world. By your power, we are more than conquerors. Thank you, Lord Jesus. Amen.

Scripture for further reading: Philippians 3:12–14; Hebrews 10:35–36; Ephesians 6:13–17.

Itchy Ears

When conflict comes, go to God first. It is good to get godly counsel, but people, even good people, often are biased with their agendas, experience, perceptions, and values, which may not always be the best guide for you at the time. Worse yet, others may tell you what you want to hear or tell you what will serve their needs. Second Timothy 4:3 says, "For the time will come when people will not put up with sound doctrine. Instead, to suit their desires, they will gather around them a great number of teachers to say what their itching ears want to hear."

Prayer: Lord, help me to discern what is right. Help me escape counsel that is uninformed, careless, and unwise. Help me to recognize wisdom from you. I come to your throne of grace, praying that you will send the right person, at the right time, and with just the right word. In Jesus' name, I pray. Amen.

Scripture for further reading: Ephesians 6:7–9 Proverbs 11:8–9; Deuteronomy 32:28–33.

_____

_____

_____

_____

_____

_____

_____

The Process

Throughout your life, God is more interested in your journey than your destination. He knows where you'll wind up in the end. He's more interested in how you respond in the best of times and in the worst of times. How you handle money when you're rich is a test. How you handle money when you're poor is a test. How you behave in good times and bad, is likewise a test. God wants to be proud of you, His beloved child, His expert creation. He wants you to lean on your Heavenly Father for strength and guidance. "For the eyes of the Lord range throughout the earth to strengthen those whose hearts are fully committed to Him" (2 Chronicles 16:9).

Prayer: Lord, I pray for those who suffer any affliction or injustice. Please give them strength, courage, and wisdom. Help me to respond appropriately, too, so that I am a part of the solution, not a part of the problem. I pray to pass each test and that you are pleased with me. Amen.

Scripture for further reading: Matthew 25:40–46; Romans 8:9–17; Deuteronomy 10:12–13.

_____

_____

_____

_____

_____

_____

_____

Stop Learning, Start Dying

Learning should be a lifelong venture. When you stop learning, you might as well be going in reverse, because everyone around you keeps moving forward. When you stop learning, it's like a prison sentence, locked away and isolated from all life has to offer. The most successful people are those who love to learn. No matter what you learn from the past, it will never tell you all you need to know for the future. Gather information from many sources. Isaiah 1:17 says, "Learn to do right."

Prayer: Father, each day, you teach me new things — things that will give me comfort, strength, and understanding. Thank you for your blessings on this journey of life. Help me to keep learning so that I'll be ready to handle the fullness of your blessings. I appreciate this wisdom, and thank you for it. Amen.

Scripture for further reading: 2 Corinthians 3:18; Jeremiah 33:3; Isaiah 48:17.

Objection Overruled

Try to be gentle with others — God's not finished with them yet. Trust that God is working in their life. Deliberately think about what is good and right in them. Practice what God has taught in Matthew 7:5: "You hypocrite, first take the plank out of your own eye, and then you will see clearly to remove the speck from your brothers' eye." Any objections you make against others are overruled by God's command to focus on your faults; then help others out of their predicament.

Prayer: Lord, when I judge others, I'm in effect saying that you're not capable of creating your magnificence in them. Neither am I your final masterpiece. Change my heart, Lord. Help me acknowledge your glory and see at least one good thing in every one. There's always something to compliment. That will help me see others the way that you see them: full of life, potential, hope, and purpose. Amen.

Scripture for further reading: 2 Corinthians 7:13–16; Romans 2:1–4; Romans 3:9–12.

_____

_____

_____

_____

_____

_____

_____

The Measure of Time

Time passes. Every day we are given a choice on how to spend time. Don't waste a second being afraid, anxious, or worried. Why be concerned about tomorrow? Anxiety is exhausting. Worry is meditating on the negative. Fear is a demon to steal joy. Cast your care on Jesus and rejoice in the favor of God, always. Measure the time of your life by the quality of how you spend it. It is God's good pleasure for you to walk with Him in everlasting joy. Isaiah 43:1 says, "Do not fear, for I have redeemed you; I have summoned you by name; you are mine."

Prayer: Lord, thank you for everything in my life — food, clothing, health, medicine, family, love, good relations, rest, abundance, air, radiant sunshine, a sense of accomplishment, and an intimate relationship with you. You gave me innumerable blessings and kindnesses. Help me remember to rejoice in you, always, and fear not. Amen.

Scripture for further reading: 1 Peter 5:7; Proverbs 12:25; Philippians 4:4.

Satan's Schemes

Be careful of Satan's schemes to promote selfishness and incite conflict. When tempted to think, act, or speak in a way that is not pleasing to God, acknowledge Him. In the middle of Satan's schemes, it is time to stay strong, do what's right, and walk in the Spirit of God's abiding love and protection. Use the resources God gave you to remain at peace, as much as possible. "Let the peace of Christ rule in your hearts, since as members of one body you were called to peace. And be thankful" (Colossians 3:15).

Prayer: Lord, protect me from Satan's schemes for conflict with others. The devil will not leave me alone, so I need to stay in your word and your presence every day. Let me be grateful for every moment of this day. I need your mighty power in my life. Amen.

Scripture for further reading: Psalm 4:6–8; Romans 5:12–21; Romans 8:12–13.

Life Is Just a Bowl of Cherries

Life is not perfect. Things don't always go the way we think they should. Your alarm clock doesn't go off in the morning, your car breaks down, or the price of gas just increased again. Try a little humor. Live and laugh at the hard times. Hard times will pass. Enjoy your life as much as you can. It's a much better choice than letting the events spoil your day. Colossians 3:7–8 says, "But now you must also rid yourselves of all such things as these: anger, rage, malice, slander, and filthy language from your lips."

Prayer: Lord, Jesus felt betrayed, misunderstood, and discouraged. The burdens He carried were more severe than anything I could imagine. Yet, He turned His problems over to you, God. When tempted to let negative feelings run rampant, help me to follow Jesus' example. Help me to overcome any scheme of the enemy and walk in joy, strength, and courage that are available in you. Amen.

Scripture for further reading: Isaiah 45:7–8; Romans 8:28; Romans 8:18–21.

_____

_____

_____

_____

_____

_____

_____

_____

Successful Strategy

As parents hope for their child's happiness and success, God also longs for your happiness and success. God has unlimited resources and would love to give you every possible blessing. The first thing is to ask God for what is on your heart. Chances are if you have an intimate relationship with God the Father, He has placed that desire in your heart because He'd like for you to live it. But the Bible reminds us, "You desire but do not have...you covet but you cannot get what you want...you do not have because you do not ask God" (James 4:2). So, if you've already asked fifty times in the last year and God hasn't answered you, what's the holdup? You wouldn't give the Maserati keys to your teenager. Nor would God turn over the keys to the universe, until you were ready to receive them. Take the best care of what He has already given you. Thank Him for every good gift. Ask God to provide you with wisdom. Tell others how your Heavenly Father has blessed you.

Prayer: Lord, Father Almighty, I thank you for your goodness and grace. I praise your holy name as the King of kings, Lord of all, and Creator of all good things. You are the master of the universe. All honor and glory are yours. In Jesus' name, I ask that you will complete your work in me. Amen.

Scripture for further reading: 1 Corinthians 15:57; 2 Corinthians 8:6–8; Colossians 3:16–17.

_____

_____

_____

_____

_____

The Potter's Clay

Just as a potter takes immense measures to clean, mold, and create a chosen vessel out of clay, God takes immeasurable care to design great beauty and purpose in you. How sad for people who rebel against God's incredible creative power and miss allowing Him to mold them into the perfect creation He has planned for them. They remain like a blob of clay. God selected you for an extraordinary and unique purpose. Cooperate with His plan for your life. First John 3:2 tells us, "Dear friends, now we are children of God, and what we will be has not yet been made known."

Prayer: Lord, I fall to my knees. I surrender my life to you. I lay my plans down and surrender to your loving will. Take my heart and mold me. May your glory unfold within my life. Make me a sweet reflection of your perfect will. For that purpose, only, will I be completely blessed. Amen.

Scripture for further reading: Proverbs 27:19; Ecclesiastes 5:18–20; 2 Timothy 2:1–7.

_____

_____

_____

_____

_____

_____

_____

_____

Love God With All Your "Mite"

The Bible says that one day, Jesus went to the temple and watched people make their offerings. Many rich people dressed in beautiful robes and contributed much money. Then, a poor widow dropped two small copper coins in the offering. Jesus told His disciples, "Truly I tell you, this poor widow has put more into the treasury than all the others. They all gave out of their wealth; but she, out of her poverty, put in everything — all she had to live on" (Mark 12:43–44). Jesus was more interested in the heart of the giver than the size of their gift. There are many ways to give of yourself to make the kingdom grow — with time, kindness, talent, energy, as well as money.

Prayer: Lord, I put all my thoughts, plans, and activities on trial before you. May my motives be pure, and my actions be pleasing to you. Help me stay focused on eternal life. In Jesus' name, I pray. Amen.

Scripture for further reading: Romans 12:3–8; Matthew 25:34–46; Deuteronomy 30:19–20.

_____

_____

_____

_____

_____

_____

Leadership Principles That Win

I imagine there are enough leadership books, that if lined up end to end, could span the world's circumference. But there is only one leadership model that has lasted for over 2,000 years, and that is from Jesus. His deep passion for serving others illustrated His leadership principles. He developed, encouraged, and challenged His disciples. He often stopped what He was doing to help those in need. He cared deeply for others, worked tirelessly, and made the greatest sacrifices for those who followed Him. "Do you not know that in a race all the runners run but only one gets the prize? Run in such a way as to get the prize" (1 Corinthians 9:24). Jesus demonstrated how to win the prize.

Prayer: Lord, you entrusted me to run my race. May I glorify you and win the prize. Amen.

Scripture for further reading: Galatians 6:9; Hebrews 13:7; Matthew 20:26; Philippians 2:4.

_____

_____

_____

_____

_____

_____

Are You Ready?

When Paul made a heart commitment to Jesus on the road to Damascus, he was not yet ready to minister to others. Paul loved Jesus passionately, but he needed to spend more time with Jesus, know Him better, and learn His ways. To lead others to the marvelous news of Christ, Paul needed to practice love, gentleness, goodness, faithfulness, encouragement, patience, endurance, and self-control. Before he could lead others to Christ, he needed to become more like Him. Becoming more like Christ pleases God. "I seek not to please myself but Him who sent me" (John 5:30).

Prayer: Lord, I too am like Paul. I love Jesus with all my heart, but when I try to minister to others, I mess things up. I need to integrate my mind with my heart. Like Paul, I need to spend more time in your presence, in your Word, and in practicing your ways. How can I please you today? Amen.

Scripture for further reading: Romans 15:14–16; Romans 12:9–13; Colossians 3:17.

_____

_____

_____

_____

_____

_____

_____

Opportunity in Challenge

With every cloud, there is a silver lining. With every storm, there is a rainbow. So too, with every challenge, there is opportunity. God created it that way. When life is out of control, time and energy are in short supply, and obstacles seem insurmountable, get ready to see God's glory. Don't respond with fear, anger, sadness, or denial. Instead, react with curiosity and wonder. God's unconditional love will help you get past adverse circumstances to find your greatest joy. "The Lord is my light and my salvation — whom shall I fear? The Lord is the stronghold of my life — of whom shall I be afraid" (Psalm 27:1)?

Prayer: Lord, some days are so hard, I don't know whether to laugh, cry, or go crazy. The Bible reminds me that you give peace in all circumstances. The Bible tells me that you will be with me in every challenge. Help me experience your splendor in every situation. Help me to face the day with wonder and excitement for all that lies ahead. In Jesus' name, I pray. Amen.

Scripture for further reading: Proverbs 29:25; Job 36:19–33; Romans 8:35–37.

_____

_____

_____

_____

_____

_____

On Fire and Full of Passion

Be on fire and full of passion for serving others in your calling. Serving is very Biblical. We are here to serve rather than be served. The devil continually tries to entice us to become self-serving gods, separated from God. Never be envious of selfish people who appear to live a life of ease, and free from care. The enemy only challenges those who are a threat to him. Never grow tired of serving. Those who love and follow Christ receive the promises of God for abundant and everlasting life. "The Son of Man did not come to be served, but to serve, and to give His life as a ransom for many" (Matthew 20:28).

Prayer: Lord, I belong to you and seek to live the life that is pleasing to you. I know living with this kind of passion makes the devil tremble. When my feet hit the floor in the morning, I want the devil to quiver, knowing that I'm on fire with a passion for serving you. Keep me from greed, selfishness, and pride. Help me to serve you better every day. Amen.

Scripture for further reading: Romans 1:1–6; Romans 7:4–25 2 Corinthians 9:10–11.

_____

_____

_____

_____

_____

_____

Chasing the Wind

There are two kinds of wisdom. The first is human wisdom, based on ideas and belief systems that change with the times. Throughout Ecclesiastes, Solomon referred to human wisdom as meaningless and a chasing after the wind. The second kind of wisdom is divine. Divine wisdom is from God and does not change. Divine wisdom is the same today, as it was yesterday, and as it will be in the future. Godly wisdom serves as a compass for living a good, pure, and satisfying life. In these times, our generation places significance on establishing laws of humanity as the guiding light. But, human wisdom will not change people's hearts to make them do what's right. Having a spiritual identity in Christ, and intimacy with God the Father is key to a transformed life. God gives His wisdom freely to those who place Him, not laws, at the center of their lives.

Prayer: Lord, may this be a generation of people who passionately follow you. Rescue this generation from the dominion of darkness and bring everyone into the kingdom of light. May we finish evangelizing the world. May the promised blessing of your presence upon all people be made manifest. Amen.

Scripture for further reading: 1 Corinthians 1:25; Romans 1:18–25; Romans 4:13–15; Romans 1:28–32.

_____

_____

_____

_____

_____

$\mathcal{A}$ $\mathcal{L}$ove $\mathcal{L}$ike $\mathcal{N}$o Other

When you turn music on, what are you likely to hear? You'll listen to love songs, including songs of new love, disappointing love, and crazy love. But the love of God is like no other. The Bible is the most excellent love letter ever written by the most celebrated author of all time. His words boldly, unashamedly, and repeatedly reveal how much you are cherished. God reveres your intimate relationship as His most prized treasure. He has counted and knows the number of every hair on your head. He thinks about you more times than there is sand in the ocean. God never withholds His words of love. His love is unconditional, intimate, and more profound than any love you'll ever experience. "I trust in God's unfailing love for ever and ever" (Psalm 52:8).

Prayer: Lord, thank you for this precious love. It is a love like no other. May our love grow dearer. Amen.

Scripture for further reading: Isaiah 43: 1–7; 1 John 4:9–10; Jeremiah 31:3; 1 John 3:1.

_____

_____

_____

_____

_____

_____

_____

Ultimate Betrayal

When there's a need to justify oneself or blame others, lookout. Playing the role of victim and villain is a defeating response because we take no responsibility in the conflict. The ultimate betrayal is not in what others do to us. The ultimate betrayal is to ourselves by not recognizing our ability to change things or give them a proper perspective. When we are not accountable, we limit our growth and proficiency. Responsible people focus on solutions. Proverbs 2:9–11 says, "Then you will understand what is right and just and fair — every good path. For wisdom will enter your heart and knowledge will be pleasant to your soul. Discretion will protect you and understanding will guard you."

Prayer: Lord, help me to be accountable. In every conversation, conflict, and encounter, I have a part. Accountability may call for an apology; it may require letting go of anger or resentment; or, a gentler response may be needed. Whatever the scenario, help me to learn what I can do to conform more closely with your plan. Amen.

Scripture for further reading: Colossians 2:1–5; Colossians 3:12–14; Philippians 4:21–23.

_____

_____

_____

_____

_____

_____

Replacement Principle

When tempted to nurse and rehearse an unpleasant incident, a better solution is forgiveness. Yes. Forgive others. Not for their sake, but yours. If you hold unforgiveness, it will eat at you like a poison, bringing anger, bitterness, resentment, and all sorts of emotions that steal your joy and eat at your soul. With God's help, you can forgive by practicing the replacement principle. Replace painful thoughts, memories, and feelings with pleasant ones. Then you can focus on what's essential: your life, joy, and future. "We will share with you whatever good things the Lord gives us" (Numbers 10:32).

Prayer: Lord, give me the grace to think on higher things. Replacing the negative with more positive thoughts, words, and actions are critical for a world in pain. By dwelling on problems, I give them too much power. Help me to focus on what is right, pleasant, and pure. In Jesus' name, I pray. Amen.

Scripture for further reading: Romans 2:12; Philippians 4:8–9; Romans 4:2–8.

_____

_____

_____

_____

_____

_____

Centered on the Wheel

Imagine a potter shaping clay on the wheel. The potter can't work with the clay unless it's centered and stable. When Christ is not the center of our lives, we remain as a blob of clay. Doing things our way is not freedom. We can't make our lives beautiful on our own. Real freedom comes from allowing the potter to mold us into something beautiful. Reading the Bible, spending time with God, and being obedient, are ways to stay centered in Him. "But now that you have been set free from sin and have become slaves of God, the benefit you reap leads to holiness, and the result is eternal life" (Romans 6:22).

Prayer: God in Heaven and of my life, guide me and protect me from getting off-kilter. When I insist on doing things my way, put me back in the center of your will. Mold me and make me what you will. Amen.

Scripture for further reading: Romans 8:22–25; Romans 6:1–7; John 3:30.

_____

_____

_____

_____

_____

_____

_____

_____

It Will Be Well With You

What is success? Is it getting up one more time than you fall? Is it scrapping and scraping to get to the top of the corporate ladder? Or is it found in having more toys than others before you die? People who are addicted to success are not enviable. There's no joy in success for the sake of success. God wants you to be successful, but not at the expense of missing a meaningful relationship with Him. Psalm 128:1–2 states: "Blessed are all who fear the Lord, who walk in obedience to Him. You will eat the fruit of your labor; blessings and prosperity will be yours."

Prayer: Lord, I pray for your hand to be on me today. Help me to be successful in everything I do, not for my glory, but for yours. Amen.

Scripture for further reading: Psalm 128:1–2; Matthew 16:26; Romans 1:14–17; Romans 9:30–33.

Let Love Sleep

Song of Songs is a book in the Holy Bible to show the value of love between a man and a woman. Song of Songs 8:4 instructs us, "Do not arouse or awaken love until it so desires." The love between a man and a woman is holy. God teaches us to wait for His perfect timing for perfect love. There's joy in finding a new love, but there's also a vulnerability to heartache. There's a natural tendency for selfishness and want. Time is needed to develop trust. When two people learn to support one another through thick and thin, trust grows. There is security in giving a relationship time to build trust.

Prayer: Lord, love can feel like a four-letter word, or it can be everything that you created it to be. Help me to learn to love and be loved. Help me to respect your proper timing. Amen.

Scripture for further reading: Psalm 33:20–22; Psalm 130:5–6; 1 Corinthians 4:5.

Adjust Your Expectations

Are your expectations for life picture perfect? Do you expect everyone to act like you, think like you, and talk like you? Do you design a plan A, and commit to an "I'm sticking to it" attitude? What happens when a friend insists on having his or her way? It's admirable to adjust your expectations. Come up with a plan B that allows for love and peace. Plan B might be better to help build a bond. The day is better when the focus is to get along, rather than insist on having your way. Besides, plan A is so dull when you consider there are twenty-five more letters in the alphabet. The Bible is full of scripture on harmony and living at peace with others. Psalm 119:9 reminds us that we can keep our motives pure by "living according to [God's] word."

Prayer: Lord, I don't want to be rigid and consumed with my schedule, plans, and me, me, me attitude. Help me to realize that if I stay flexible and open, there will be occasions for serendipitous experiences and great opportunities. Amen.

Scripture for further reading: Deuteronomy 2:7; Exodus 13:21–22; 2 Chronicles 17:5–6.

_____

_____

_____

_____

_____

_____

_____

What Truth Do You Base Your Life On?

What is the truth? It can be a fact, or it can be a belief that you accept as truth. In ancient times people believed the world was flat; that was their truth. Today many of our truths are what our politicians, scientists, or the media tell us. Those truths may not be fact, but we believe them, so they become truth for us. Everyone bases their lives on reality. But what is your reality? Is everything that your instructors tell you the truth? Is everything you read on the internet truth? Truths are based on one's perception. But it's not gospel. John 17:17 says, "Sanctify them by the truth; your word is truth."

Prayer: Lord, the Bible teaches that we are in this world, but as Christians, we are not of it. I hear and see the ways of the world, and am saddened by it. I don't want to practice the ways of the world. We are in desperate need of truth. Have mercy on us, Lord. I am, through you, set apart, saved, and here to live a life separate from worldly ways. Thank you for showing me the best way. Teach me the truth. Amen.

Scripture for further reading: 1 John 3:18; 2 Timothy 2:15; John 1:14–17; Psalm 25:5; Psalm 119:160.

_____

_____

_____

_____

_____

When Bad Things Happen

How could a good and loving God allow bad things to happen to good people? But that's just what He does. Sometimes people get angry that God allows bad things to happen. Know that He does not cause bad things to happen. God understands our anger, but He is pleased when we continue to grow in faith. God does work all things for good for those who love and follow Him. Sometimes, He uses that pain to make us stronger; sometimes, He uses that pain for us to show others how to get through it. We may never know the answer while we walk on this earth. God uses every pain and every sorrow for the ultimate good. Your pain is His pain. God collects every tear in Heaven and restores every heartache. For now, God wants us to grow in faith and trust in His wisdom. John 3:15 says, "that everyone who believes may have eternal life in Him." The time we spend on earth is but a whisper, just the blink of an eye, compared to the time in eternity. Today we have a choice to walk in faith or doubt.

Prayer: Lord, forgive my unfaithfulness when I doubt your wisdom. I don't know why people must suffer, why there is sorrow, or why good people must experience pain. Help me grow in faith. Teach me how to comfort those who are in momentary pain and suffering. Help me follow you faithfully, trusting in you and your eternal glory. Amen.

Scripture for further reading: Psalm 91:14–16; James 1:12; 2 Corinthians 4:17; 1 Peter 5:10.

_____

_____

_____

_____

Purpose, Passion, and Provision

You are no accident. God had a plan for your life before He created you in your mother's womb. God makes each person unique and special. We are wonderfully made. Why did God make your friend great at math, or your sister excellent at tennis, but you have no talent at either? It's OK if you're not a mathematical genius or a star athlete. God had something exceptional planned for you. Trying to do something that God didn't design for you to do is like a washing machine wishing to be a dryer, or a thumb hoping to turn into a pinkie. Isaiah 45:10 says, "Woe to the one who says to a father, 'what have you begotten?' or to a mother, 'what have you brought to birth?'" Be happy and celebrate who you are. Be satisfied with your gifts.

Prayer: Lord, I welcome today with hope and joy. I will celebrate every opportunity to discover and improve the gifts and talents you've given me. I turn my day and everything in it, over to you. I put my faith in you to bring me to an abundance of purpose, passion, and provision. Amen.

Scripture for further reading: Proverbs 20:5; Isaiah 46:10–11; Ephesians 2:10.

_____

_____

_____

_____

_____

The Best Is Yet to Come

Imagine Michelangelo's sense of accomplishment upon completion of his glorious 65-foot masterpiece on the ceiling of the Sistine Chapel. Envision the powerful emotion of Donatello gazing at the beauty of his profoundly inspiring bronze statue of David. The artist is inspired and enchanted with extreme passion and joy in creating his masterpiece. So, it is with our Creator. God has enormously extravagant capabilities for creating the most magnificent of all creation in the universe. What an astonishing masterpiece: a living, seeing, hearing, smelling, touching, tasting creation of beauty, full of thought, energy, and words, together with a full range of emotion and giftedness. What beauty in you. If the artists' work is marred, he doesn't throw it away. He paints over it until he finds perfection. The sculptor doesn't give up on the first try. He reshapes the clay to make something pleasing to him. So, it is with our Creator. But our God is greater than any other creator, no matter how prominent. The most enchanting part of our Creator's design is freedom of choice; what a marvelous God. If we remain moldable, by walking with Him, cooperating with Him, and loving Him, He will create in us more than we could hope, think, or imagine. "For you created my inmost being; you knit me together in my mother's womb. I praise you because I am fearfully and wonderfully made; your works are wonderful; I know that full well" (Psalm 139:13–14).

Prayer: Lord, thank you for your great love and a deep passion for creating life in me, inspired by your excellence. It is magnificent to have access to your unlimited power, fullness of joy, and breath-taking radiance. May I cooperate with you and walk in your redeeming grace. Father, I look forward to this journey and fulfillment of your joy in me. The best is yet to come. Amen.

Scripture for further reading: Proverbs 31:25–26; Genesis 1:27; Ephesians 4:24.

More Like Jesus

Jesus understood the value of a day's work. He understood the difficulty of working with others, meeting deadlines, and being challenged beyond human limits. Jesus was God, yet He was not ashamed to do a man's work. When challenged, think about how Jesus would do the task. Would he be more patient? Listen more than He would speak? Be kinder? Gentler? Would He find more joy in the work? Would He choose His words more carefully? "Dear friends, now we are children of God, and what we will be has not yet been made known. But we know that when Christ appears, we shall be like Him, for we shall see Him as He is" (1 John 3:2). What a glorious occasion to be more like Jesus.

Prayer: Lord, today, I am so far from being like you. When I try in my efforts, I set myself up for failure. I am so far from being perfect. On too many occasions, I react negatively. Sometimes I say hurtful things. When I'm feeling inadequate, how should I respond? Where do I start? I'm learning that these feelings and emotions are your loving and gentle way of saying, "Child, you need to come up higher in this area; let me help you." Thank you for loving me so much to change me, from glory to glory, and not stay stuck in childish ways. Amen.

Scripture for further reading: Romans 12:1–2; 2 Corinthians 5:17; Romans 6:11; 1 John 2:6.

_____

_____

_____

_____

_____

Devil, You Can't Steal My Joy

Despair is a tool the enemy uses to steal all hope. When living in despair, it's hard to find solutions. People may think of easy solutions to your circumstance, but God alone has the answer when life gets hard. Be honest with God. Put the truth about your doubts, fears, sorrow, and confusion out there, and ask Him to reveal the truth. Even if you can't trust the circumstance, you can trust God over the circumstance. "The Lord is near to all who call on Him, to all who call on Him in truth. He fulfills the desires of those who fear him; he hears their cry and saves them" (Psalm 145:18–19).

Prayer: God, in you, hope is alive. I put my faith in you. Help me to be patient in suffering. I seek you in my despair and ask for and receive your guidance so that I may again find joy, and my joy may be made complete. In Jesus' name, I pray. Amen.

Scripture for further reading: John 16:24; Micah 7:7; James 5:7–11.

Tough Times

Everyone experiences pain. How are we to handle it? What possible purpose could a loving God have for allowing pain? Job knew. In verses 23:10–11, he said, "But He knows the way that I take; when He has tested me, I will come forth as Gold. My feet have closely followed His steps; I have kept to His way without turning aside." Gold is purified as it is washed, filtered with fire, ground into smaller particles, then ground again, and finally pulverized. Ever feel like that? Those are the times we question the very nature of God. But it is right during those times, that we become moldable, our character is made pure, and our motives perfected. It is only then that our loving God can shape us into something precious, something of value. Through the process, God is with us to see that we become more like Jesus, who is pure perfection.

Prayer: God, it is hard to go through painful times. It is hard to know the purpose. It is hard to understand how to respond. It is hard. Thank you for being with me and taking all my pain and using it only for good. Thank you for restoring me to wholeness, better than before. Thank you for loving me enough to create pure perfection. Amen.

Scripture for further reading: 2 Corinthians 13:5–7; Jude 1:17–25; 2 Chronicles 7:14.

_____

_____

_____

_____

_____

A Love Like No Other

Where you live, the age you live in, and the people in your life are not coincidental. God chose this place and time for you and all those characters in your life, to make a beautiful story. He equips us and guides us and gives us free will to create an even better story. He tells us so in the Bible, His love letter to us. "The Lord appears to us in the past, saying: 'I have loved you with an everlasting love; I have drawn you with unfailing kindness'" (Jeremiah 31:3). Because of our mutual loving relationship with God, we need to set time aside, praying, worshiping, and praising Him. Tell God how much you love Him and appreciate Him. It pleases God when we give Him the glory for every good thing in our lives.

Prayer: Lord, I belong to you. May you abide in me, and I abide in you. Bring me to a quiet place and shut out all thoughts and distractions so that in this silence, I can focus on the Holy Spirit within me, and experience being in the radiance and beauty of your loving presence. Amen.

Scripture for further reading: 1 Thessalonians 5:18; Romans 9:7–8; Romans 12:1–2; Hebrews 13:20–21.

One With the Father

Do you always feel God's presence? First John 5:13 tells us that, "I write these things to you who believe in the name of the Son of God so that you may know that you have eternal life." It does not say, "so you may hope and feel that you have eternal life." You can look forward to eternal life. How can you be sure? Do you remember the first time you experienced or even had a glimpse of the tremendous love of God? Selah, or pause and think about that. As divine love grows, you know He is with you. You know He wants only good for you. You know that He abides in you, and you abide in Him. You know you become one with the Father. God desires this kind of personal relationship with you.

Prayer: Lord, thank you for revealing the depth of your love. I seek you and rejoice in your presence. Amen.

Scripture for further reading: Galatians 1:1–5; Colossians 1:24–27; Colossians 3:18–21.

Long Term Gains Outweigh Short Term Benefits

Foolishness. There was a man named Esau who gave up his family's inheritance for a bowl of stew. In a very impulsive bargain, Esau gave up his right as head of the family to satisfy an immediate need of hunger. He was the firstborn, which gave him the right to lead the family and gain the bulk of his father's estate. But Esau lived dangerously. Instead of taking his rightful place as the head of the family, he chose to be a hunter. How could he inherit anything if a wild animal killed him? How many of us relinquish future benefits to satisfy immediate desires? Instant gratification makes for poor decision making. "See that no one is sexually immoral, or is godless like Esau, who for a single meal sold his inheritance rights as the oldest son" (Hebrews 12:16).

Prayer: Lord, sometimes, my life is a mess. I forget that tough times are just moments in time — they will pass. Help me apply wisdom, considering long-term potential outcomes, rather than giving into immediate gratification. Amen.

Scripture for further reading: Colossians 3:1–3; Hebrews 12:11; Philippians 4:10–13.

_____

_____

_____

_____

_____

Time Well Spent

Time is measured in seconds, minutes, hours, and days. But more importantly, time is measured by the quality of it. Time is measured as good or bad, by how we choose to spend it. The Bible tells us to make the best use of our time. Colossians 4:2–3 says, "Devote yourselves to prayer, being watchful and thankful. And pray for us, too, that God may open a door for our message, so that we may proclaim the mystery of Christ, for which I am in chains."

Prayer: Lord, come into my heart, my day, my life, and my future. Open doors that I may boldly profess that there is nothing more perfect, pure, and holy than time spent with you. Amen.

Scripture for further reading: Ephesians 6:18; John 17:4; Ephesians 5:16; Micah 6:8.

_____

_____

_____

_____

_____

_____

_____

_____

_____

When I've Made a Mess of Things

Have you ever said or done something to hurt someone, only to wonder afterward how you can make things right? Walking away after you've hurt someone only causes the problem to fester. As soon as possible, talk to God about it, confess your mistake, and ask God to help you change the situation. Listen and be obedient. Do you need to admit fault to the person you offended? Or do you accept the consequences, change your attitude, or ask them to forgive you? Matthew 5:9 says, "Blessed are the peacemakers, for they will be called children of God."

Prayer: Lord, help me to be sensitive to promptings of the Holy Spirit so that I don't offend others. When I hurt others, make me aware of the offense. Forgive me and help me to learn from this error. I ask for reconciliation and request that you will act to remove any hostilities that exist. Mend our relationship with love, joy, unity, and gladness. Amen.

Scripture for further reading: 2 Timothy 2:24–26; 2 Corinthians 5:18–19; Proverbs 10:15.

_____

_____

_____

_____

_____

_____

_____

Hope

Hope is the desire for something good and anticipation of its fulfillment. Romans 5:2 states, "we boast in the hope of the glory of God." This verse clearly emphasizes that we should put our hope in God. Hope is the spark that sets God's glory blazing. All hope perishes for those who forget God, but those with faith in God are secure, and their hope is alive. Those who hope in the Lord will not live in shame. Put your hope in Jesus.

Prayer: Lord, you are a gentle yet powerful God. You soothe my soul and enrich every experience. The more that I am aware of you, the more I am blessed with hope and fulfilled in every way. Amen.

Scripture for further reading: 1 Peter 1:3; Proverbs 11:7; Psalm 42:11; Ephesians 1:18.

Relentless Pursuit

I love to sit in my backyard and spend time in the silence to hear God's voice. I admire the splendor of His remarkable creation of nature. My peace and joy are sometimes disrupted by the continuous barking and howling of my neighbor's dogs, every time a leaf drops, someone passes by, or when the wind blows. When situations are harassing, or people oppose you, how can you continue to find peace and do what is right? It's only with God's help. You can pray, of course. You can continue to say what is helpful and constructive. You can seek counsel or support from others who are spiritually mature. Explore all options. But above all else, relentlessly pursue peace. Proverbs 16:7 says, "When the Lord takes pleasure in anyone's way, He causes their enemies to make peace with them."

Prayer: Lord, help me find peace, beyond what I am, by myself, capable of. Pursuing peace always involves risk. Do for me what I can't do for myself. Open the doors of our hearts to live in harmony with everyone. Amen.

Scripture for further reading: Ephesians 2:14–18; 2 Corinthians 13:11; James 3:17.

_____

_____

_____

_____

_____

_____

Give Them Hope

Do you ever feel helpless to console someone who is suffering? It is no accident that you are there for them at this moment. You are in peoples' lives for a reason, and that reason is to give them hope. How can you give hope? Sometimes it's a hug, a smile, or a word of encouragement. Sometimes it's sharing a similar hardship that you've experienced. Sharing your experience and letting them know the success, joy, or happiness on the other side of their pain is precisely the hope they need. "And we know that in all things God works for the good of those who love Him, who have been called according to His purpose" (Romans 8:28). Give others hope. What an honor that God trusts you to do His work.

Prayer: Lord, on this earth, we are assured of having difficult times. Yet we also know, with confidence that you are with us, and provide all we need to endure with patience until we see your glory. Give me grace, too, to help others who are suffering, and give them hope. Amen.

Scripture for further reading: 2 Corinthians 9:6–9; Romans 5:5; Romans 15:3; Romans 8:24–29.

_____

_____

_____

_____

_____

_____

_____

Two to Tango

As sure as it takes two to tango, there are two sides to every story. Every argument, every confrontation, and every disagreement involves differences of perception. So, ask yourself: What are the ways I contributed to the conflict? Was I reckless with my words? Was I too sensitive? Did I gossip, control, or talk badly about someone? Am I being motivated by pride, fear, power, money, prestige, or favor? Acknowledging your part is not taking all the responsibility for the conflict. Others have an obligation, too. As you are accountable for your part in a dispute, God can work to change the situation and restore peace within your soul. "Who may ascend the mountain of the Lord? Who may stand in His holy place? The one who has clean hands and a pure heart.... They will receive blessing from the Lord and vindication from God their Savior" (Psalm 24:3–5).

Prayer: Lord, you tell me that if I keep doing good, you will exalt me in due time. If I refuse to take any responsibility, or if I refuse to forgive, I am giving Satan an advantage in my life. Whatever it takes, I don't want to give the enemy a foothold for chaos, confusion, evil, suffering, or pain. I will run to you, stay in the word, and pray without ceasing to remain strong in you. When I want to tell someone off, help me to stay strong in you. When I get offended, help me to stay strong in you. When I want revenge, help me to stay strong in you. Amen.

Scripture for further reading: Proverbs 16:32; Proverbs 14:29; Matthew 5:22; Psalm 37:8–9.

Can You Give a Testimony?

After a test, you can walk away with a testimony, or you can walk away moaning. The difference is in your response. Sure, you can withdraw and become aggressive, but a better answer is to pursue peace. Withdrawal and aggressive behavior negatively affect a person's physical and mental well-being and do nothing to resolve the situation. Someone who actively seeks peace, on the other hand, will experience more desirable outcomes. There are many ways to begin the process of pursuing a peaceful solution. The apostle Paul was continually tested but made it a practice to stay in dialogue. "To all in Rome who are loved by God and called to be his holy people: Grace and peace to you from God, our Father and from the Lord Jesus Christ" (Romans 1:7). He treated others with respect but was honest and firm in his convictions. He found common ground: when in Rome, he would do as the Romans would do. Find something to agree about, even if it's just an agreement to disagree. Try to understand why others are misbehaving. It's worth it. If it were not for Paul's efforts, two-thirds of the world would not now know of the hope, goodness, and love of Jesus. What a testimony to the pursuit of peace. Stay in peace during the conflict, as God is using it as an opportunity for you and your adversary to learn something new, and that is pleasing to Him.

Prayer: Lord, thank you for the apostle Paul's example to pursue peace. If Paul had exhibited aggression or withdrawn from his mission, the world would not experience the glorious outcome. What a difference one man made for all the world, just by practicing peace. I'm so thankful to remain in peace. Amen.

Scripture for further reading: 2 Corinthians 12:14–21; Galatians 1:13–16; Ephesians 2:2–10.

The Habit of Solitude

When people try to convince you to compromise, get away for a while, and spend time in solitude. How long has it been since you spent even an hour in solitude? Solitude provides clarity, renewal, and revelation. It's time to gain strength and confidence. It's a time to spend at the throne of grace. It's a time to hear the sweet whispers of God's voice. Jesus did that, and often. In solitude, you give yourself time to come to your senses. First Corinthians 15:33–34 says, "Do not be misled: 'Bad company corrupts good character. Come back to your senses as you ought.'"

Prayer: Lord, I ask to develop the habit of breaking away and spending time with you. I cherish time with you. Fellowship with you is rewarding. Amen.

Scripture for further reading: Philippians 4:15; Mark 1: 35; Philippians 6:46; Matthew 14:23; Matthew 26:39; Luke 5:6; Luke 9:18.

_____

_____

_____

_____

_____

_____

_____

_____

Smarter Goals

In the story *Alice's Adventures In Wonderland,* written by Charles Lutwidge in 1865, Alice was at a crossroads. She came upon the Cheshire Cat and asked for directions. Since Alice didn't know where she was going, the cat couldn't tell her which way to go. That is the perfect example of a person without a goal. Without goals, there's no direction. Without goals, it's easy to get lost. We don't know what tomorrow brings, but with humility, start seeking God's will for your life. Galatians 3:3 says, "Are you so foolish? After beginning by means of the Spirit, are you now trying to finish by means of the flesh?" Ask God what matters most. Set your goals, diligently plan for better results, and allow Him to direct your steps.

Prayer: Lord, I diligently seek you and your will for my life. Would you direct my path? Time is infinite, but it seems there's rarely enough time to get everything done. Help me set correct goals so that I don't get sidetracked or waste time headed in the wrong direction. Amen.

Scripture for further reading: James 4:13–15; Proverbs 16:9; Proverbs 21:5.

The Legacy of a Journal

As a child, I would watch my grandfather read his torn and tattered Bible. He'd write the Scripture down on paper, and reflect on what he'd written. What a legacy for grandchildren. I didn't realize then, but he was building truth into his life. Here's a suggestion:

- Identify a need and look in the index of your Bible to research truth on the matter.
- Write down scripture verses so that it becomes ingrained in your heart and mind.
- Repeat the verses out loud as a mantra, memorizing it for when you need it again.

"Remember the day you stood before the Lord your God at Horeb, when He said to me, 'Assemble the people before me to hear my words so that they may learn to revere me as long as they live in the land and may teach them to their children'" (Deuteronomy 4:10). Relying on the word of God is a guaranteed method to find strength during times of need.

Prayer: Lord, help me to seek your instruction for every area of life. Help me to pass this legacy to future generations. Continue to inspire and teach us how to live. May we live our lives on the foundation of your truth. Amen.

Scripture for further reading: Philippians 2:25–30; Jeremiah 30:2; Psalm 119:21; Psalm 102:18; Joshua 1:8.

_____

_____

_____

Anger Is Dangerous

It makes sense that the word, anger, is a derivate of the word, danger. Anger provokes dangerous things that you're later ashamed of, things you can't take back. Anger gives Satan a foothold in your life and keeps you from living the victorious life God desires. Instead of getting angry, fully reflect on the situation to discover a fuller perspective of the case. Here's how:

- Write down every detail of the situation: the place, the time, the people.
- Why did you get angry, what were you deprived of, and how did it make you feel?
- What would you say to a friend if they had gone through a similar experience?
- What could happen to get better results?
- What did you learn? God would not allow it to happen if there wasn't something to learn.
- Next, study from the Bible to discover what God says about the situation.

"Refrain from anger and turn from wrath; do not fret — it leads only to evil" (Psalm 37:8).

Prayer: Lord, anger is an emotion that should cause me to run to you. Help me to replace anger with understanding. Amen.

Scripture for further reading: Proverbs 29:11; Proverbs 15:18; James 1:19–20; James 4:1–2.

_____

_____

_____

Make Disciples of All Nations

God has given us the commission to make disciples of all nations. He gives everyone unique gifts to fulfill His command in unique ways. You may worry, "Am I too aggressive? Not aggressive enough? Will I offend someone?" God will give us the words, opportunity, money, time, everything necessary to complete the task. "Therefore, go and make disciples of all nations, baptizing them in the name of the Father and of the Son and the Holy Spirit, and teaching them to obey everything I have commanded you. And surely, I am with you always, to the very end of the age" (Matthew 28:19–20).

Prayer: Lord, help me to approach each person with wisdom. Unite us to finish the work you have commissioned us to complete. Amen.

Scripture for further reading: Ephesians 2:19–22; Ephesians 3:2–6; Colossians 1:21–23.

An Heir to the Throne

People buy into the value system of the world. How you look, what you do, and who you are related to, seem to be important matters to the world. We often use these worldly perceptions to value ourselves, but when we do, we always sell ourselves short. The enemy will tell you, "You're not good enough. You always goof up. You don't look as good as your neighbor." God has a different way of looking at your worth and value. Galatians 4:6–7 says, "Because you are sons, God sent the Spirit of His Son into our hearts, the Spirit who calls out, 'Abba, Father.' So you are no longer a slave, but God's child; and since you are His child, God has made you also an heir." Know this: you are a child of our God, a prince/princess. Every day, remind yourself of what the King of kings has to say about you.

Prayer: Lord, although I am not perfect, I am your child. On days I'm not feeling confident, remind me of who I am. Remind me of whose I am. Remind me that I am the very child of God, and I belong to you. Amen.

Scripture for further reading: Romans 8:14–17; Romans 8:29–34; Romans 9:13–21; Galatians 3:23–29.

_____

_____

_____

_____

_____

_____

Angels Among Us

God did not create us to be alone. I have friends I'm convinced are angels. We support, nurture, encourage, and sharpen one another. We make unforgettable memories together, celebrate our friendship during good times and bad, and love one another through thick and thin. Friends are like angels in every season of life. Hebrews 1:14 says, "Are not all angels ministering spirits sent to serve those who will inherit salvation?" Thank God we have one another.

Prayer: Lord, thank you for being my strength when I am weak. You are my source to bring comfort, forgiveness, rejoicing, and laughter. Thank you for your goodness in providing ministering spirits. Amen.

Scripture for further reading: Romans 15:1; Romans 12:15; 2 Corinthians 1:3–5; Galatians 6:2; Colossians 3:13.

_____

_____

_____

_____

_____

_____

_____

_____

_____

_____

Fighting Battles

We are all fighting a battle of some kind. God has a plan for your life, and so does the devil. Pray for wisdom to know which plan to battle and which to embrace. If you fight every conflict on your knees, you win. First Timothy 1:18–19 says, "I am giving you this command in keeping with the prophecies once made about you, so that by recalling them you may fight the battle well, holding on to faith and a good conscience, which some have rejected and so have suffered shipwreck with regard to the faith."

Prayer: Dear Lord, in life, we wrestle against powers of darkness. Help us to put on the armor of God. May we keep the faith, persevere, and never shrink back from the challenge. Amen.

Scripture for further reading: Ephesians 6:11–12; 1 Timothy 6:12; 2 Timothy 4:7; Hebrews 10:39.

_____

_____

_____

_____

_____

_____

_____

_____

You Are Full of It

Living by the power of the Holy Spirit is also referred to as being filled with the Spirit. The Holy Spirit lives within every Christian, but not every Christian is filled with the Spirit. If Christians are full of themselves, rather than of the Holy Spirit, the Holy Spirit cannot empower them. Self-directed Christians produce ordinary results as their own devices limit them. But the difference between ordinary and extraordinary is the extra that is available through the Holy Spirit's indwelling. Acts 1:8 reminds us of this new empowerment: "But you will receive power when the Holy Spirit comes on you; and you will be my witnesses in Jerusalem, and in all Judea and Samaria, and to the ends of the earth."

Prayer: Lord, may I be less full of myself; instead, fill me with your Holy Spirit. I am thankful for the extraordinary things the Holy Spirit can do when I stop trying to do life on my own. I thank you for every good thing: food, clothing, shelter, transportation, provision, health, medicine, family, love, good relations, rest, relaxation, luxuries, abundance, air, fragrant smells, radiant sunshine, work, a sense of accomplishment, prayer, and a relationship with you. Thank you for innumerable blessings and kindnesses. May the burdens of those less fortunate be replaced with blessings from the Holy Spirit. Amen,

Scripture for further reading: John 3:30; 1 Corinthians 3:16–23; Galatians 3:7–14.

_____

_____

_____

_____

Mile Wide Relationships

There are only a handful of people in life you will be able to call a friend. There is a big difference between a friend and an acquaintance. The relationship with most people is strictly intellectual or casual. With technology, there are more opportunities for communication, but the relationships developed online are a mile wide and an inch deep. You can talk, talk, talk, talk, talk, but when things get tough, you can't rely on them. Develop a more profound relationship at the heart level. A true friend is one who loves, through thick and thin. The sweet friendship of a true friend refreshes the soul. Proverbs 17:9 says, "Whoever would foster love covers over an offense, but whoever repeats the matter separates close friends."

Prayer: Lord, a friend, is a gift from you. I give you thanks for the sweet friends in my life. Amen.

Scripture for further reading: Proverbs 27:9; Proverbs 18:24; Proverbs 13:20; Proverbs 17:17; Proverbs 22:24–28; John 15:13; Ecclesiastes 4:9–10.

_____

_____

_____

_____

_____

_____

_____

Love Is Hard Work

It is not easy to love everyone God puts in your life. And yet, that is what God commands you to do. It's easy to love the loveable; anybody can do that. It's not so easy to love others with difficult personalities. Some people are just mean spirited. Does God want you to love them? How about people who are in love with themselves? What about people who always seem to be out to get us? God calls us to love others beyond what we can do on our own. God first loved us when we were in sin. Because God's generous and amazing love overflows for us, we can find within ourselves love enough for others. We can look at them through God's eyes, to find compassion or discover something good about them. Because of God's abundant love, we can look at others as an unfinished product of God's astonishing creation. God wants us to love others through their hard times, their challenges, and their imperfection. Romans 5:5 says, "And hope does not put us to shame, because God's love has been poured out into our hearts through the Holy Spirit, who has been given to us."

Prayer: Lord, help me to love others as you love them. I'll need help here. Amen.

Scripture for further reading: 1 Samuel 16:7; 1 John 4:7–21; John 15:12.

_____

_____

_____

_____

_____

_____

Why Is There Sorrow in the World?

No one is exempt from sorrow. Sorrow comes from a loss: loss of a dream, a job, or a relationship. Experiencing grief is an opportunity to see the hand of God at work. How is that possible? God grows near to those who are broken-hearted. It says so in the Bible. Those who know God know that is true. Any time you're in sorrow, remind yourself that you'll soon see the victory; you'll quickly see God's glory. You'll experience the peace that surpasses all understanding. You'll see the miracle-working hand of God bring healing, comfort, and restoration. Psalm 34:18 says, "The Lord is close to the brokenhearted and saves those who are crushed in spirit."

Prayer: Lord, please stay close to me today. Be with friends and family, and all those who are suffering. I need you every hour, every minute, and every second of every day. Thank you for being the Father, who will never leave me nor forsake me. Amen.

Scripture for further reading: John 16:20–24; Hebrews 12:5–11; Psalm 91:1–16.

_____

_____

_____

_____

_____

_____

Stages of Grief

It's hard to understand why people react differently to grief. One rule of thought is that people process grief in different ways. People respond because they are going through various stages of grief. There are many ways people experience heartache. Some react with anger; others with denial; many become depressed. Most people experience all the emotions of grief at one point or another in their grieving process. But no matter how we exhibit our sorrow, God is there with us. We know God is with us just as He was with Jesus as He wept with Mary and Martha after their brother Lazarus died. Those who are friends with God are comforted knowing we can bear our soul to Him, knowing He will be with us, no matter how or when we face our grief. Lamentations 3:31–33 says, "For no one is cast off by the Lord forever. Though he brings grief, he will show compassion, so great is his unfailing love. For he does not willingly bring affliction or grief to anyone."

Prayer: God, you are amazing. I think about the extent of your great love. How much more you must grieve than we grieve. How much more are you hurt by injustice than we are hurt? Your love is deep, and your compassion is deeper. Your love is perfect, Lord God Almighty. Amen.

Scripture for further reading: Romans 8:35–39; 1 John 1:3–4; Isaiah 41:13.

_____

_____

_____

_____

_____

The Sweet Aroma of Knowing Him

Do your friends see Christ in you? When they think about you, do they think, "There's a Christian." Let's hope so. It's okay that you're not perfect. Only Jesus was perfect. Your friends should see the fruits of the Spirit in you, which are patience, love, gentleness, kindness, goodness, faithfulness, self-discipline, peace, and joy. Second Corinthians 2:14 says, "But thanks be to God, who always leads us as captives in Christ's triumphal procession and uses us to spread the aroma of the knowledge of Him everywhere."

Prayer: Lord, I pray that I please you in everything I do. I pray that I become more like Jesus so that others may see you in me. Amen.

Scripture for further reading: Matthew 6:1–4; John 13:34–35; Ephesians 5:1.

_____

_____

_____

_____

_____

_____

_____

Nothing Can Separate Me From Your Love

You can love God because He first loved you. Nothing can separate you from God's incredible love: not your mistakes, not the past, not the present, not the future; not even the schemes of the devil can separate you from His love. God's love is unfailing, everlasting, and unconditional. Often, we mistakenly search for that kind of love in others, but human love is not capable of producing such love. Philippians 2:1–2 says, "Therefore if you have any encouragement from being united with Christ, if any comfort from His love, if any common sharing in the Spirit, if any tenderness and compassion, then make my joy complete by being like-minded, having the same love, being one in spirit and of one mind." As we unite in God's love, we become one in Him.

Prayer: Father, I need your love, the love that only comes from knowing you personally. Knowing about you is different from knowing you. I am grateful for your love and will never separate from it. Amen.

Scripture for further reading: 1 Corinthians 6:17; John 14:20; Genesis 1:26.

_____

_____

_____

_____

_____

A Pure and Just God

God loves you so much, but He also loves justice. Because God is pure and just, there is not a sin or crime that can go unpunished. Just as light cannot live in darkness, God cannot live where there is injustice. His love is so profound that He sent His only Son, who was without blemish, to take our sin, suffer the consequence of our sin, to give us eternal life and be one with the Father. Love so amazing requires only one thing: that we ask for and receive His forgiveness for anything that grieves the Holy Spirit. Revelations 3:19–20 tells us, "Those whom I love I rebuke and discipline. So be earnest and repent. Here I am! I stand at the door and knock. If anyone hears my voice and opens the door, I will come in and eat with that person, and they with me."

Prayer: Lord, I am in awe of you. The extent of your love humbles me. Forgive me for any thought, word, or deed that has grieved the Holy Spirit. I receive your forgiveness and thank you for the marvelous gift of salvation. You take my sin and give me redemption. Thank you, God, Father Almighty. Let your power, glory, and majesty reign forever and ever. Amen.

Scripture for further reading: Matthew 5:8; Leviticus 11:44–45; Ezekiel 36:25–27.

Power Source

The Holy Spirit is the power source for godly living. A refrigerator has no power on its own. To function, it must draw energy from its source, electricity. The ability to live an abundant Christian life comes from continually drawing from our source, which through God's grace, is the power of the Holy Spirit working in and through us. Access to God's grace is always available if we choose to access it. Walking in infinite love and purity gives us access to unlimited possibilities available through the Holy Spirit's power. "For this reason I kneel before the Father, from whom every family in heaven and on earth derives its name. I pray that out of His glorious riches He may strengthen you with power through His Spirit in your inner being, so that Christ may dwell in your hearts through faith. And I pray that you, being rooted and established in love, may have power, together with all the Lord's holy people, to grasp how wide and long and high and deep is the love of Christ, and to know this love that surpasses knowledge – that you may be filled to the measure of all the fullness of God. Now to Him who is able to do immeasurably more than all we ask or imagine, according to His power that is at work within us, to Him be glory in the church and in Christ Jesus throughout all generations, for ever and ever. Amen" (Ephesians 3:14–21).

Prayer: Lord, help me to walk in purity and your infinite love. I pray for the fullness of knowing and loving you. I pray for your grace to access the power available for me through the Holy Spirit. May this knowledge and understanding permeate throughout the world and define future generations. In Jesus' precious name, I pray. Amen.

Scripture for further reading: 2 Peter 3:18; Acts 4:33; 2 Corinthians 9:8; 1 Corinthians 1:4–8.

Just as I Am

Many people use imperfect Christians as an excuse not to become Christians. But that's what it is — an excuse, not a reason. We are made perfect by the sacrifice that Jesus made on the cross. He took our sins, so that if we follow Him, our sins may be erased and remembered no more. We are not made perfect by our good works. I will always let somebody down, but God won't. Peter, one of Jesus' disciples, talked and laughed and spent time with Jesus. Jesus loved Peter, even though Peter continually disappointed Him. Peter was impulsive and denied Jesus three times. So, don't be discouraged if you are not the perfect reflection of Jesus. God's not finished with you yet. "Therefore, my dear brothers and sisters, stand firm. Let nothing move you. Always give yourselves fully to the work of the Lord, because you know that your labor in the Lord is not in vain" (1 Corinthians 15:58).

Prayer: Lord, give me a heart that is full of zeal to see your glory. There are areas of my life that need perfecting, but I trust that through your love, I am made whole. Your disciples sinned. They were not perfect. Yet, you chose them for your purpose and loved them. That makes me know that you love me, just as I am, in all my imperfection. I am not perfect, but I'm thankful that I know the One who is. Amen.

Scripture for further reading: Mark 10:18; Ecclesiastes 7:20; Philippians 22:8.

_____

_____

_____

_____

_____

No Worries

At the last supper, Jesus' disciples were troubled by His comments to Judas Iscariot. In response to their troubled hearts, Jesus gave them peace. First, Jesus told them that there was a place in heaven for them. Then He told them the Holy Spirit would guide them. Finally, Jesus blessed them with peace saying, "Peace I leave with you; My peace I give to you; I do not give as the world gives. Do not let your hearts be troubled and do not be afraid" (John 14:27).

Prayer: Lord, I thank you for your example to sow peace when a friend's heart is troubled. Let me share the sweet word of God, so that it may remove fear, anxiety, and doubt. May your divine word remove the barriers that obscure the omnipotence of Christ, within every troubled heart. In Jesus' name, I pray. Amen.

Scripture for further reading: 2 Corinthians 12:6–10; John 14:1–14; John 14:15–31.

_____

_____

_____

_____

_____

_____

_____

_____

Relationships and Results

Jesus was God, but He humbled Himself to do man's work. In your work, do it to the best of your ability, and do it for God. In relationships, fervently strive to build trust, empower others, give recognition, and make great memories. Serve God by serving others. Give God the glory for blessings in relationships and work. First Kings 2:3 reminds us to "observe what the Lord your God requires: Walk in obedience to Him, and keep His decrees and commands, His laws and regulations, as written in the Law of Moses. Do this so that you may prosper in all you do and wherever you go."

Prayer: God, I cling to your providence and grace. Teach me more fully your truths, so that I may walk by the light of them and live in the radiance of your presence. The Bible has every answer and gives guidance in every situation. I pray for increased godliness in my relationships and my work. In Jesus' name, I pray. Amen.

Scripture for further reading: Genesis 39:2–6; 2 Corinthians 8:22–24; Luke 16:10–11; Proverbs 16:3.

_____

_____

_____

_____

_____

_____

_____

_____

Seek Solutions

If you dwell on a problem, it will distort your vision. The more you focus on issues, the larger they become. Know that our God is bigger than your problems. Know that when God trusts you in a challenge, He also has a solution to fulfill His purpose. God has the answers. So, "Let us then approach God's throne of grace with confidence, so that we may receive mercy and find grace to help us in our time of need" (Hebrews 4:16). God trusted Moses to lead the Israelites out of Egypt and into the promised land. So why did it take the Israelites forty years to make an eleven-day trip? Instead of seeking God to guide them, they focused on their problems. Instead of trusting the God of hope, they put their trust in things. Instead of thanking God for saving them from bondage, they grumbled and complained. God is the light in our darkness, our help in time of need, and the solution to every need.

Prayer: Lord, I know the depths of your love are more magnificent than I can comprehend. Yet you yearn to draw me closer, not to love me more, but to bless me more. What a blessing available to me. Remind me to focus on the power available in you instead of problems. You are my light, my help, my answer, and my Lord. Amen.

Scripture for further reading: 2 Timothy 3:16–17; Isaiah 65:24; Hebrews 4:16; Psalm 18:30.

_____

_____

_____

_____

_____

Parents Can Help You

Proverbs 6:22 talks about honoring your parents: "When you walk, they will guide you; when you sleep, they will watch over you. When you awake, they will speak to you." Let your parents help you. They are a gift from God to show the way to God. They've been put in your life to love you, and they're there for your success.

Prayer: Lord, please bless my family and me. I know the level of blessings you desire to give us require greater wisdom and grace, so that we may learn to stand in strength, power, and authority. Instill in us, your wisdom and grace. Protect us from every harm. Lead us into a deeper love and appreciation for one another, through Christ Jesus, our Lord. Amen.

Scripture for further reading: Colossians 3:18–21; Genesis 6:9–10; 1 Chronicles 16:43.

_____

_____

_____

_____

_____

_____

_____

_____

_____

_____

Parents Can Be Irritating

Sometimes parents are so irritating — but honor them. Even if you disagree with your parents, you can learn from them. They're interested in you not making the same dumb mistakes they made. "Children, obey your parents in everything for this pleases the Lord" (Colossians 3:20). Right or wrong, you can honor your parents by not speaking badly to them or about them. Forgive them. Comfort them. Understand them. When we honor our parents, we are honoring God's sovereignty and purpose in giving them to us. Above all else, praise God, the Father.

Prayer: Lord, I will open my mouth and speak boldly: I am your child. You know me. You know everything I say or do, and everything I will ever say or do. You see the purpose for every season in my life, and where you are taking me. Your plan is good because you are good. I am no surprise to you. Thank you, God, for understanding, mercy, direction, discipline, and love. I am not perfect, but trust you will guide me in your ways. Amen.

Scripture for further reading: Ephesians 6:1–4; 1 John 3:1; John 10:28–30; Proverbs 3:11–12; Proverbs 15:5.

Good Company

Choose your friends wisely. Second Peter 3:17 says, "Be on your guard so that you may not be carried away by the error of the lawless and fall from your secure position." You need to keep good company for three reasons:

- The people you associate with influence you.
- People perceive who you are by the company you keep.
- How others treat you, to no small extent, is predicated on who your friends are.

Desire the company of people who have pure hearts. They're the ones with excellent reputations and admired by others.

Prayer: Lord, you suffered at the hands of others and were misunderstood by many. Yet, during those times, you listened to them, offered comfort, and overlooked their offenses. I ask that you bring godly friends into my life and develop in me that same beautiful character. Amen.

Scripture for further reading: Galatians 5:7–10; Proverbs 22:24–25; Proverbs 5:13–20.

_____

_____

_____

_____

_____

_____

_____

Imposing

Do you always insist on having your way? It's not Biblical to impose your wishes on others. The Bible teaches that we should treat others the way that we would like to be treated. Always choose to be thoughtful and considerate by respecting others' space, wishes, and time. They will think more highly of you if you do. "Remind the people to be subject to rulers and authorities, to be obedient, to be ready to do whatever is good, to slander no one, to be peaceable and considerate, and always to be gentle toward everyone" (Titus 3:1–2). The Bible confirms the benefits of practicing a more thoughtful approach when interacting with others. Daniel gained favor for himself and future generations from the harshest of kings by being gracious. Paul found support with the Romans by respecting their customs. Imposing on others will cost you honor and favor.

Prayer: Lord, you created me to do something special. I will need honor and favor to accomplish the assignment. May I be more thoughtful and considerate of others. Put a guard over my mouth. Remove pride and arrogance from my heart. Show me a better way. Amen.

Scripture for further reading: Romans 14:1–10; Amos 5:11–13; Colossians 2:20–23.

Believing a Lie

Don't believe everything you read and hear. The news, your neighbor, the internet, and books in school are all wrought with personal agendas, limited perspectives, and misunderstanding. Don't believe a lie. Pray to discern the truth. Be particularly discerning with information about God and the written word of the Bible. First John 4:1–3 warns, "Dear friends, do not believe every spirit, but test the spirits to see whether they are from God because many false prophets have gone out into the world. Here's how to recognize the Spirit of God: Every spirit that acknowledges that Jesus Christ has come in the flesh is from God, but every spirit that does not acknowledge Jesus is not from God. This is the spirit of the antichrist, which you have heard is coming and even now is already in the world."

Prayer: Lord, I pray that I, my loved ones, and all the children of this nation and the world, cling to you. May we experience your grace and majesty. Help us discern what is right and true. Help us to follow you, to know you better, and choose the path to eternal life. In Jesus' name, I pray. Amen.

Scripture for further reading: 1 John 4:1; Galatians 1:6–9; 2 Timothy 4:1–5; 2 Corinthians 6:14–18; 2 Corinthians 11:12.

Keep Love Alive

We can't live in the light of God if darkness fills our souls. God allows us to choose our path: to walk in His grace or to walk in our wickedness. The wicked receive kindness, but it doesn't change their hearts. They can't see, understand, acknowledge, or appreciate the fullness available through the love of Christ. In Ephesians 3:19, I pray that you "know this love that surpasses knowledge — that you may be filled to the measure of all the fullness of God." The blessings available in the fullness of God include His majesty, grace, goodness, miracles, power, happiness, favor, and eternal life. How do you access the fullness of God? Wherever there is love, you will find the love of Christ. Keep love alive.

Prayer: Lord, how your heart must ache when you offer so much, but we choose our ways. Thank you for not abandoning us when we turn our backs on you. Thank you for giving us patience and kindness as you eagerly long to bring us into the light. You placed me here, at this time, and with these people for a purpose, and that purpose is to speak the truth. Help me to show others the love of Christ and the fullness of life with you. Let your light shine brightly through us, that we spread it all over the world. All honor and glory are yours, Father. In Jesus' name, I pray. Amen.

Scripture for further reading: Isaiah 26:10; Romans 8:38–39; 1 John 4:7–21; Hebrews 6:10.

High Road

We should strive to reach spiritual maturity, but I'm not sure that any of us fully arrive before God takes us home. Even Jesus, as a human, was subject to limitations of human knowledge. The Bible tells us that Jesus grew in wisdom of divine law and increased in favor with God and man. We can move toward greater spiritual understanding by taking the high road. Reject what is wrong, and choose what is right. Follow what is pure and pleasing to God. It's not always the easy way, but it always leads to a better place. Hebrews 12:14–15 instructs us to, "Make every effort to live in peace with everyone and to be holy; without holiness, no one will see the Lord. See to it that no one falls short of the grace of God and that no bitter root grows up to cause trouble and defile many." Don't live with less than God's best.

Prayer: Lord, I pray to be strengthened by the Holy Spirit, to grow in wisdom and grace, and to complete the work you prepared for me to do. Help me to reject everything sinful and evil. Help me to choose what is right and pleasing to you. May the power of the Holy Spirit flow through me and operate within me. Help me to grow in knowledge, strength, and character. Amen.

Scripture for further reading: Hebrews 10:35–36; Hebrews 11:6 Hebrews 12:11; Genesis 11:31–32; Isaiah 7:15.

The Rich Exchange

It is God's will for us to receive His grace. We can't earn it; if we could, it would not be grace. We certainly don't deserve it; Christ obtained it for us. In our limited understanding, we sometimes reduce the meaning and power of grace. Grace is more than getting a sense of well-being and taking care of ourselves. Grace is so much more. God's grace is the ultimate expression of His love and is given freely for those ready to receive it. Grace is the supernatural power to open our blind eyes to see the glory available through Jesus Christ. The entire Bible reveals the glory that is in Christ, so that our joy may be everlasting. Grace is divine power evidenced by the apostles to bear witness and convert the multitudes to Christian faith. The fullness of grace is to experience divine beauty, and everlasting joy made manifest through Him. The only way of receiving His divine grace through the Holy Spirit is to confess your sins, ask forgiveness, and invite Him into your life. May His grace be abundantly revealed in you and through you.

Prayer: God, There are areas of my life that grieve the Holy Spirit. Reveal them to me Lord so that I can name them one by one and receive forgiveness. I accept you as my Lord and Savior. Reveal to me those thoughts, words, attitudes, and actions that are not pleasing to you. Help me to change my ways so that I may receive your divine grace and live in the glory that is available in Christ Jesus, my Lord. Amen.

Scripture for further reading: John 1:12; John 15:11; John 17:5; John 17:17; John 17:24; Romans 8:29; Colossians 3:10.

_____

_____

_____

Stewardship

Remember the saying, "A penny saved is a penny earned?" The same principle applies to other resources as well. Money, time, and energy are all scarce commodities. It's important to God that we are good stewards of what He has given us. Why should God give us more when we're not faithful with what He has already provided? Stewardship requires both faith and effort. Obedience requires that we take the initiative and are eager to be faithful in the administration of our affairs. God blesses those who do what is right, in the eyes of the Lord, and the eyes of man. First Corinthians 4:2 says, "Now it is required that those who have been given a trust must prove faithful."

Prayer: May I honor you, Lord, with all that you have so richly provided. You are a God of unlimited resources, but desire my obedience in managing my time, money, and energy. Give me your grace, God, to faithfully execute all my affairs with enthusiasm, and according to your will. Amen.

Scripture for further reading: 2 Corinthians 8:16–21; Psalms 24:1; Matthew 25:21–29; Proverbs 21:20.

Make a Difference Into Eternity

How you spend your time and money, tells God a lot about you. Do you spend your time and money doing good for others? Does your spending reflect reverence for God? These things bring about results that last into eternity. Time and money wasted can never be found again. Think twice before you spend time and money on pleasures that last just for the moment. "The Lord will watch over your coming and going, both now and forevermore" (Psalm 121:8). Spend time, money, and energy in a way that pleases our Lord.

Prayer: Lord, when I am running short on time, money, and energy remind me that I am your beloved child and blessed with unlimited resources. Help me, Lord, to turn away from greed and worldly desires and become more generous than ever. Help me to use all resources in a manner pleasing to you. Amen.

Scripture for further reading: Romans 12:15; 1 Corinthians 9:6-7; 1 Peter 4:16.

_____

_____

_____

_____

_____

_____

You've Got the Power

Proverbs 21:23 says, "Those who guard their mouths and their tongues keep themselves from calamity." Think about what you say before you say it. There is power in words. If you say negative things, it opens the door for sorrow or destruction. Angels in Heaven respond when positive words are spoken. Not sure that's true? Why else would God tell us the key to entering His gates is with praise and thanksgiving? You get what you say. Spend the day grumbling and complaining, and get more of the same. Make it a better day by complimenting others, giving thanks for every good thing, and sharing joy. You've got the power!

Prayer: I pray to speak positive things into my life and the lives of others. May I thank you ten times a day for blessings at the moment. May I thank you for your majesty. Remind me that I am a child of God. I am a speaking spirit with power in my words. Amen.

Scripture for further reading: Philippians 2:14–16; Ephesians 4:29; Matthew 12:36; Proverbs 18:21.

How Did You Say It?

The Bible says, "A gentle answer turns away wrath, but a harsh word stirs up anger" (Proverbs 15:1). A soft answer is always better than a sarcastic one. How something is spoken is just as important as what is said. Words reflect a persons' heart. People draw closer to those who habitually speak words that are acceptable, pleasing, and kind. Gracious speech is a delightful and rare quality.

Prayer: Lord, give me knowledge and discernment in choosing my words. I pray for the grace to use words that are beneficial, refreshing, and true. Give me a pure heart to speak words that bring honor and favor. Keep me from uttering words that offend, condemn, and inflame. Amen.

Scripture for further reading: 2 Corinthians 7:8–13; Psalm 141:3; Matthew 12:37; Proverbs 17:27–28.

Never Be Abrasive

You are never persuasive when you're abrasive. Ephesians 4:29 reminds us, "Do not let any unwholesome talk come out of your mouths, but only what is helpful for building others up according to their needs, that it may benefit those who listen." A top biomedical engineer, well known within his industry, strived for perfection. He worked tirelessly on developing equipment to diagnose medical problems. However, his social demeanor was abrasive. He dismissed ideas of colleagues, antagonized his superiors, and slandered his competition. As time passed, his abrasive demeanor alienated all those who might otherwise have supported his work. He was ultimately forced into retirement. The product would have been a tremendous benefit to many, but no one ever got to see it; what a loss.

Prayer: Father, help me to use words that are prudent and full of promise. Help me find the right word, at the right time, for the right purpose. May I treat others with respect, keep peace in all situations, and walk in grace and kindness. Amen.

Scripture for further reading: Proverbs 16:24–30; Colossians 3:8; Proverbs 15:4.

Gossip

Proverbs 16:28 tells us, "A perverse person stirs up conflict, and a gossip separates close friends." Sometimes people gossip because they are hurt, looking for understanding, or just want to vent. But gossip always comes back to haunt you — it makes you look bad later. Talk to God about it, instead. Learn to vent vertically.

Prayer: God, put a guard over my mouth and keep me from ruin. If I am upset, I pray to demonstrate self-control. Let me pause and seek you during the confusion. I don't want to dwell on the incident or speak about it to others. Give me peace and understanding to go on with my day. In Jesus' name. Amen.

Scripture for further reading: James 1:26; Matthew 15:11; Isaiah 55:11; Proverbs 13:3.

_____

_____

_____

_____

_____

_____

_____

_____

_____

Talk to God About It

Talk to God about everything. He wants to be in every part of your life. It pleases Him. Philippians 4:6 says, "Do not be anxious about anything, but in everything, by prayer and petition, with thanksgiving, present your requests to God." Make God your constant companion today. Tomorrow, wake up with the same conviction, to share your day with Him. Each day that you walk with God, you'll experience greater joy and fulfillment.

Prayer: Lord, when I am hurt or angry, let me rest in your presence. Aligning my thoughts with scripture, despite how I feel, activates spiritual power. If I choose to release any unforgiving, unholy, or impure thought, I am choosing instead to receive from your infinite possibilities for good. Thank you, Lord, for this kind of freedom. Amen.

Scripture for further reading: Colossians 4:6; Psalm 19:1–14; Psalm 141:1–10; Hebrews 13:15.

_____

_____

_____

_____

_____

_____

_____

_____

Forgiveness

When people hurt you, forgive them quickly. These people are in your life for a reason, and that reason is for your benefit. They are there to teach you what you otherwise wouldn't learn. Perhaps you'll learn patience, or your faith will grow. You will discover that while people will give up on you, your Father in Heaven never will. Don't be bitter in trials; be better. Thank God for wisdom. Matthew 6:14–15 says, "For if you forgive other people when they sin against you, your heavenly Father will also forgive you. But if you do not forgive others their sins, your Father will not forgive your sins."

Prayer: Lord, I need the grace to forgive. You saved me from darkness and forgave my sins. Give me the grace to extend grace to others. As I offer forgiveness, I am increasing spiritual truths and the Holy Spirit's power in my life. Amen.

Scripture for further reading: 2 Corinthians 12:9; Colossians 1:13–14; Mark 11:25, Psalm 63:12.

Good in Every Season

God promises good in every season. God does not allow anything to happen that will not blossom into the fullness of the ultimate good. It's just hard to see at the time. The perfection of our souls comes from struggles and storms. Be patient while God prepares you for your role in eternity. Second Corinthians 7:10–11 says, "Godly sorrow brings repentance that leads to salvation and leaves no regret, but worldly sorrow brings death. See what this godly sorrow has produced in you: what earnestness, what eagerness to clear yourselves, what indignation, what alarm, what longing, what concern, what readiness to see justice done. At every point, you have proved yourself to be innocent in this matter."

Prayer: Lord, I pray for courage as I begin this day, for there is work to be done. You are in control. Renew my strength. Help me to replace fear and pain with hope in you. Thank you for your faithfulness to love and comfort us in times of adversity. Amen.

Scripture for further reading: Isaiah 41:10; Psalm 73:26; James 1:1–13; Romans 5:15.

_____

_____

_____

_____

_____

_____

Uniqueness

Galatians 5:24–26 says, "Those who belong to Christ Jesus have crucified the flesh with its passions and desires. Since we live by the Spirit, let us keep in step with the Spirit. Let us not become conceited, provoking, and envying each other." You are an original creation with unique gifts and abilities. There is no one else like you. Be thankful for who you are. You are God's handiwork, created in Christ Jesus to do good works which God prepared in advance for you to complete.

Prayer: By your grace, God, I live in the fullness of your love. I am a wonderful creation made by you, the great Creator. I am a work in progress. I value myself as I am. I continue to grow and excel in unique qualities and skills each day. Help me to be patient with myself, knowing that you are not finished with me yet. Fulfill your glory in me, Lord Jesus, I pray. Amen.

Scripture for further reading: Proverbs 31:10–31; Song of Songs 4:7; 1 Peter 3:3–4; Colossians 2:10.

_____

_____

_____

_____

_____

_____

_____

Authenticity

Be true to yourself. Whether you're shy, bold, funny, or serious, don't be superficial. Be proud of who you are. Only when you allow your personality and talents to flourish, will you find real success. People spend too much time trying to improve areas they're not talented in, or changing areas they're weak. A better strategy is to focus on areas of strength, celebrate them, and build upon them. God said, "Before I formed you in the womb, I knew you, before you were born, I set you apart" (Jeremiah 1:5).

Prayer: Lord, help me to be true to who I am. Thank you for my gifts and talents. Help me to flourish and grow. I praise you, Lord, for the excellent opportunities to use these gifts and talents in marvelous ways, and to do your work for your Kingdom. Amen.

Scripture for further reading: Hebrews 5:12–14; Psalm 92:12; 1 Corinthians 13:10; 1 Timothy 4:11–15.

I Am What I Am

First Corinthians 15:10 says, "But by the grace of God, I am what I am." Be at peace with yourself. Be content with your body, your face, and your personality. Before you can truly love others, you must first be satisfied with yourself, exactly as you are today.

Prayer: Lord, I am a unique creation designed by you. I pursue dreams, keep active in events, and love people that are right for me. I do what I do because it's specific to me. This wisdom has given me a healthier mindset. Thank you for this perspective, Lord. Thank you for this unique and radiant life. Amen.

Scripture for further reading: Colossians 2:7; Philippians 1:6; Colossians 1:10.

_____

_____

_____

_____

_____

_____

_____

_____

_____

_____

_____

Motives

Do you do good deeds to be recognized by others? Or, do you do good deeds to serve God and His children? God knows your heart. He knows your motives. Proverbs 16:2 reminds us, "All a person's ways seem pure to them, but motives are weighed by the Lord."

Prayer: Lord, look at my heart. If there is anything that is displeasing, perfect me. Purify my heart. Check my motives as I press ahead to win the prize in the race for which you called me. Help me to discern what is best, pure, and blameless. In Jesus' name, I pray. Amen.

Scripture for further reading: 2 Corinthians 8:8–9; Philippians 3:13–14; Philippians 1:9–11.

_____

_____

_____

_____

_____

_____

_____

_____

_____

_____

Perfection

Second Corinthians 3:18 promises that we "are being transformed into His image and ever-increasing glory, which comes from the Lord, who is the Spirit." Even though God can transform us instantly, He develops us little by little. It takes a lifetime to become all God created you to be. Be patient with yourself and others. God is not finished with you yet.

Prayer: Lord, I pray to do my work in faith, excellence, and integrity. May I be the apple of your eye, and grow in character, until I accomplish the perfection found in you. Amen.

Scripture for further reading: 2 Corinthians 7:10–13; 2 Corinthians 9:4–5; Isaiah 40:31.

_____

_____

_____

_____

_____

_____

_____

_____

_____

Can You Learn to Love the Unlovely?

Matthew 5:44–46 says, "But I tell you, love your enemies and pray for those who persecute you that you may be children of your Father in heaven…If you love those who love you, what reward will you get?" When you run into unlovable people, remind yourself that these are the ones who need love the most.

Prayer: Lord, what a remarkable feat. I need help with this, Lord. I know that you are not finished with them yet, nor are you finished developing character in me. Help me to see others as you see them. Help me love them and show compassion as you love them and show compassion. Amen.

Scripture for further reading: Romans 12:14–16; Philippians 2:1–3; Matthew 9:35–38.

_____

_____

_____

_____

_____

_____

_____

_____

Unity

Psalm 133:1 says, "How good and pleasant it is when God's people live together in unity." Know that love grows when we share it. Love is not selfish, arrogant, or prideful. Love says, "What can I do for you?" Always treat brothers and sisters with love, respect, and dignity.

Prayer: Lord, thank you for good relations. Each day relations are challenged and tested. I don't take good relationships for granted. I pray that you will continue to show me ways to reduce conflict, validate and respect others, and at the same time, remain firm in my convictions. Help me to learn to live at peace with everyone. Help me to recognize and celebrate the uniqueness of each person. Amen.

Scripture for further reading: 1 Peter 4:10; 3 John 1:8; Hebrews 10–24; 1 Corinthians 1:10.

_____

_____

_____

_____

_____

_____

_____

_____

God of Love and Peace

Romans 12:18 says, "If it is possible, as far as it depends on you, live at peace with everyone." Sometimes finding peace means that you must swallow your pride. Sometimes that means you must give in or let something go. You are blessed, as you cooperate with others, instead of fighting. God encourages us all to live in love and peace.

Prayer: Lord, help me to see others as you do. In the world, power, position, and prestige, attract people. Help me to regard others, not from a worldly point of view, but see them from your perspective. Help me acknowledge others as being loved, chosen, and sanctified by the Creator of the universe. I love peace and harmony. Viewing people with a more divine perspective helps me to live in harmony. Thank you, Father, for this understanding. Amen.

Scripture for further reading: 2 Corinthians 5:16–21; 2 Corinthians 13:11–14; Ephesians 4:1–6.

Promote Peace

Proverbs 12:20 promises that "Deceit is in the hearts of those who plot evil, but those who promote peace have joy." Is there anyone right now that you need to make peace with? Ask God for reconciliation and then go to that person to start the process of promoting peace. Start by seeking common ground. If reconciliation is not the answer, ask God that everyone receives the Holy Spirit and forgiveness of sins.

Prayer: Lord, help me to understand what others are going through so that I can do my part to bring reconciliation. Help me to do my part. Lord, I ask to settle the matter. If this is not possible, I ask that you do, what only you can do, in the process of bringing wholeness. Soften my heart and help me to forgive. Amen.

Scripture for further reading: 2 Corinthians 13:11–14; 2 Corinthians 6:14–18; Ephesians 2:14–18.

_____

_____

_____

_____

_____

_____

_____

_____

Respect

Treat people with respect, and they will always be your friend. Romans 12:10 encourages us to, "Be devoted to one another in love. Honor one another above yourselves." God created all people differently; for reasons and purposes, we may not understand. Regardless of what we might think of them because of those differences, God commands that we give respect to everyone.

Prayer: Lord, please unite me with loved ones and strengthen our relationships. May we share a faith-filled awareness of your compassion, love, and peace in delicate times. With your help, Lord, I ask that we continually support one another with loving prayers. Amen.

Scripture for further reading: Romans 13:1–7; 1 Thessalonians 4:9; Colossians 3:11.

_____

_____

_____

_____

_____

_____

_____

_____

_____

Learn About Yourself

Is there anyone right now that is particularly difficult to get along with? Be thankful for them. Yes. Every person in your life is there for a purpose. You learn about yourself through your experience with them. Are you patient or impatient? Are you caring or insensitive? "I will give you a new heart and put a new spirit in you; I will remove from you your heart of stone and give you a heart of flesh" (Ezekiel 36:26). As you deepen your spiritual walk, you will learn more about yourself. Through your experiences with other people, you'll develop the fruits of the spirit: peace, patience, love, joy, self-control, faithfulness, gentleness, goodness, and kindness.

Prayer: God, help me to deepen my spiritual walk so that I may become more like you, and grow closer to you. Amen.

Scripture for further reading: 1 Timothy 1:13–17; Romans 8:1–39; Luke 5:32; 1 Corinthians 6:11.

Special Needs of Others

In serving others, we learn greater patience, understanding, kindness, and endurance. Who do you know in need? Who needs compassion, advice, knowledge, sympathy, or a helping hand? Second Corinthians 1 3–4 says, "Praise be to the God and Father of our Lord Jesus Christ, the Father of compassion and the God of all comfort, who comforts us in all our troubles, so that we can comfort those in any trouble with the comfort we ourselves receive from God." When others are troubled, we can give them the same comfort God has given us.

Prayer: Lord, when I minister to others, help me to share Psalm 42:5, which says, "Why, my soul why are you downcast? Why so disturbed within me? Put your hope in God for I will yet praise Him, my Savior and my God." Amen.

Scripture for further reading: Job 32:6–7; Proverbs 11:14; Proverbs 20:18; Proverbs 19:20; Colossians 1:28.

Joy Versus Happiness

Psalm 95:2 says, "Let us come before Him with thanksgiving and extol Him with music and song." When you are discouraged, write down terrific things God has done for you in the past. We can be joyful for so many amazing things we see and hear. Do you have a home, a bed, fresh water? If so, you are rich by world standards. Lift your spirit by thanking God for each of the extraordinary experiences you've encountered with Him. It works.

Prayer: Lord, turn my sorrow into joy. Joy is my strength. The proverb that states, a cheerful heart is a good medicine, is undoubtedly true. Thank you, God, for richly providing for my enjoyment. Thank you for teaching me to focus on blessings instead of sorrow. Amen.

Scripture for further reading: John 1:4; 1 Timothy 6:17; Nehemiah 8:10; Ecclesiastes 3:12–13.

Joyful Soul

Happiness comes from events or circumstances, but joy is eternal and comes from the Spirit of God. Second Corinthians 4:16–18 says, "Therefore we do not lose heart. Though outwardly we are wasting away, yet inwardly we are being renewed, day by day. For our light and momentary troubles are achieving for us an eternal glory that far outweighs them all. So, we fix our eyes not on what is seen, but on what is unseen, since what is seen is temporary, but what is unseen is eternal." God richly provides.

Prayer: Lord, you are the song in my life. I know that it is you who carries me through each day. When I put my faith and trust in people, even good people, they can't give me what I long for. My hope and joy are in you alone. Amen.

Scripture for further reading: 1 Timothy; 3 John 1:4; Proverbs 17:22; Ecclesiastes 3:12; Nehemiah 8:10.

Celebration

Knowing the Lord makes a night and day difference in life. Know the peace that surpasses all understanding, every time you decide to turn your life over to Jesus. In a world of injustice, war, and greed, peace is elusive. But Jesus promises that we can have peace, in John 14:27, which says, "Peace I leave with you; my peace I give you. I do not give to you as the world gives. Do not let your hearts be troubled and do not be afraid." In a world of shocking brokenness and sorrow, surprise the world with the love and splendor available to us, and through us, in our Lord, Jesus Christ.

Prayer: Lord, thank you for the promises of joy in my life. I rejoice and give thanks to you for every good thing. I make it a choice to recognize and receive a life full of peace and joy. Help me stir up the gift of praise and thanksgiving. Help me be a blessing to others who are in need. Help me unlock the celebration of life in the name of Jesus. Amen.

Scripture for further reading: 1 Peter 1:8–9; 1 Thessalonians 5:16–18; Malachi 4:2; Psalm 32:7.

_____

_____

_____

_____

_____

_____

_____

Patience Shows Self-Control

Proverbs 15:18 reminds us that, "a hot-tempered man stirs up conflict, but the one who is patient calms a quarrel." If you are patient, you won't say or do something you'll be sorry for later. The devil tries to steal the joy that God wants for you. The devil knows what irritates you and places those things in front of you to take your happiness. The enemy knows what triggers your anger and fear. Learning patience is one way to keep joy. Patience, peace, and joy are from God. When angry, take ten. Think of ten blessings to be thankful for at this moment. If that doesn't work, count a hundred blessings. Wait to speak or act until you can calm down.

Prayer: Lord, I will need help with patience. When I practice patience, I am more like you. Patience is what you desire from me. Forgive me when I am not patient. You promise that you will display your power in me in areas that I am weak. Help me to focus on eternal things. God, you deserve all the glory for the grace of peace, patience, and self-control. In Jesus' name, I pray. Amen.

Scripture for further reading: 2 Timothy 1:7; Proverbs 25:26; Colossians 3:1–25; Romans 8:6; John 16:13.

_____

_____

_____

_____

_____

_____

Radiance

There is a choice in conflict, and that is to be right or to be kind. We should always choose to be kind. Being right is highly over-rated. Second Peter 1:5-7 says, "For this very reason, make every effort to add to your faith... godliness, and to godliness, mutual affection; and to mutual affection, love." Be a light in this dark world. Shine before others with the wonder and goodness of Jesus. Be kind.

Prayer: Lord, your radiance is alive within me. My part in your divine plan is to make the right choices. Help me to be kind and shine in the lives of others. Forgive me when I fall short and insist on being right instead of kind. I have a choice, and making the right choice pleases you, fills me with radiant joy, and supports my ongoing physical and mental well-being. Fill me, Lord, with radiant life. Amen.

Scripture for further reading: Psalm 3:45; Daniel 12:3; Philippians 2:13; 2 Corinthians 3:18.

_____

_____

_____

_____

_____

_____

_____

Now Is the Time to Make a Difference

The past, present, and future are all connected by time. Each moment in time is linked to eternity. How we spend that time can be measured by the quality of it. Being kind is the little difference that makes a big difference into eternity. Proverbs 11:16 promises that "A kindhearted woman gains honor." Kindness is a spiritual gift. It should be practiced by every believer, for God's glory.

Prayer: Hello, Father, I know that I appreciate when people show kindness toward me. Yet in these numbered days, people show less and less kindness toward one another. Forgive me, Lord, on days when I'm too busy, so stressed, or in such a hurry that I don't stop to show respect, give a kind word, or be more thoughtful. Give me a heart of wisdom to show kindness to others and shine for your glory. Amen.

Scripture for further reading: 2 Peter 3:8–9; Colossians 4:5–6; Ephesians 5:15–17; James 4:13–17.

Reward

A kind act is often its own reward. Proverbs 11:17 says, "Those who are kind benefit themselves, but the cruel bring ruin on themselves." We should make every effort to be kind, not only in God's eyes but also in everyone's eyes. When others are suffering, kindness is the key that brings God's glory into the situation. When we choose to do right and be kind to others, we are showing unbelievers what Christians should be like, and we are modeling the example for our Christian friends to imitate.

Prayer: Lord, I know that I am blessed when I choose to do right. Please strengthen me to do right, seek justice, defend the oppressed, take up the cause of the fatherless, and show kindness to all. I thank you for your blessing and the fulfillment of joy in my life. Amen.

Scripture for further reading: Genesis 4:7; Deuteronomy 6:18; Romans 7:21; 1 Corinthians 6:12.

Worship Him

It's important to be kind to all of God's creatures, great and small. My mother always told me, "Do at least one nice thing for someone every day." Service is admirable; loving others is a commandment. We should also remember not to be distracted from what is most important. In Luke, the story of Martha and Mary tells us that Martha worked so hard in service that she neglected Jesus in the process. Mary, on the other hand, spent all her time loving and adoring Jesus. Martha was upset that Mary wasn't helping in the food preparation. The Lord said, "Martha, Martha, ...you are worried and upset about many things, but few things are needed — or indeed only one. Mary has chosen what is better, and it will not be taken away from her" (Luke 10:41–42). Loving our Lord is the most beautiful and powerful thing we can do. Make a conscious decision to spend time in your day, soaking in the love of the Father, and loving Him.

Prayer: Lord, give me wisdom to practice your two great commandments: to love others, and to worship and serve you with all my heart, mind, and soul. I praise you, Lord, with gladness and come before you with a joyful heart. I love you, Lord, and invite you to come into my life. You are my Savior. Thank you for your love and grace. Amen.

Scripture for further reading: Romans 5:1–2; Philippians 4:4–7; Daniel 7:27; Revelation 14:7; Revelation 19:10.

Let Them Know You Care

In John 21:16, Jesus said to Peter, "Do you love me? ... Take care of my sheep." Jesus lives in us. Our behavior should reflect living in the love we share in Christ. We are a community of believers instructed to show respect, hospitality, and support to help others find their way. For as many as possible, as often as possible, as much as possible, let others know you care. If you love Jesus, take care of His sheep.

Prayer: Lord, help me to think of others more; help me to consider their needs, their feelings, their hopes, and their dreams. I know it pleases you when I think of others. By serving others, I am serving you. You set us apart to serve you, and the result should be a changed life. We are called saints because of your overflowing love. Help me to be your eyes, hands, and feet. I pray this in Jesus' name. Amen.

Scripture for further reading: 1 Thessalonians 2:9–12; 1 Thessalonians 5:12–14; Romans 12:14–16.

Love

Do you know the depth of God's unspeakable love for you? He loved you to the cross. Imagine you are walking along the winding path outside of Jerusalem. Do you see the drops of blood in the dirt along the road where Jesus walked so many years ago? You reach the top of the hill to see Him there; His arms stretched wide on the cross. And He whispers, "This is how much I love you." Ephesians 3:19 says, "and to know this love that surpasses knowledge — that you may be filled to the measure of all the fullness of God." God's love is too beautiful to be measured.

Prayer: Father, I know that you love me more than all your creations. Your love is too beautiful for words. Your love is displayed throughout the world. I confess my sins and ask your forgiveness. May I be cleansed and receive the awesome power of your love in my life. Amen.

Scripture for further reading: Psalm 119:64; Psalm 36:5–6; Psalm 107:8–9.

_____

_____

_____

_____

_____

_____

_____

Love Everlasting

Everyone wants to be loved. We search for love, long for love, and sometimes make fools of ourselves because of love. But human love is conditional. Human love says, "I'll love you as long as you make me happy." God's love is unconditional and everlasting. God's love never fails. "See what great love the Father has lavished on us, that we should be called children of God. And that is what we are. The reason the world does not know us is that it did not know Him" (1 John 3:1). There is no other love like His.

Prayer: Lord, thank you for your unconditional love. You love me in all my unloveliness. Regardless of whether I'm having a good day or a bad day, regardless of whether I'm at my best or worst, irrespective of whether I'm living according to your plan or making plenty of mistakes, you love me, unconditionally. I need and cherish your love. Amen.

Scripture for further reading: Jeremiah 31:3; Romans 5:5; Psalm 36:7; 1 John 4:9–10.

_____

_____

_____

_____

_____

_____

_____

Hungry for Love

Do you long to be loved? The greatest happiness in life comes from knowing that you are loved. When you hunger for affection, remember that the King of the universe loves, values, cherishes, and prizes you. First John 4: 9–10 says, "This is how God showed His love among us: He sent His one and only Son into the world that we might live through Him. This is love: not that we loved God, but that He loved us and sent His Son as an atoning sacrifice for our sins." God delights in you. His love endures even when we're not so lovable. Be refreshed, perfected, and made whole in Him. His love is like no other.

Prayer: Lord, I am far from flawless, but I am perfected and made whole in your love. I thirst for you, Lord Heavenly Father. Amen.

Scripture for further reading: 1 John 4:10; Hebrews 7:25; 1 Chronicles 16:34; Zephaniah 3:17.

_____

_____

_____

_____

_____

_____

_____

_____

_____

Balance

When I was young, I was overwhelmed at times by evil in the world, that slithered into my childhood innocence. My mother would tell me to close my eyes and picture the prettiest place I could imagine. When I did, I was amazed at the peace that came over me that helped balance the pain. Sometimes, I would envision a walk on a beach. The vision was so real; I could almost feel the sand between my toes. Other times, I imagined walking through a beautiful garden and was sure I could smell the sweet fragrance of the colorful flowers. These refreshing visions helped me to get through tough stuff and find balance. Second Peter 3:17 says, "Be on your guard so that you may not be carried away by the error of the lawless and fall from your secure position." God gives us beautiful things. Take hold of them and be grateful for them, always, even in the darkest times.

Prayer: Father, in your presence, is fullness of joy. You did not create me to live a life full of worry, pain, and suffering. There is an option. I can turn every concern over to you, trust that you are working out solutions, and know that you are helping me excel each day. Choosing to place my confidence in you, I can enjoy every blessing and continue fellowship with the King of Glory. Praise to you, Lord, Jesus Christ. Amen.

Scripture for further reading: Psalm 27:4; Ecclesiastes 3:1–8; Mark 6:31; Luke 10:38–42; Psalm 16:11.

Praise God

"Pride goes before destruction; a haughty spirit before a fall" (Proverbs 16:18). Satan was created perfect and in a position of privilege. But he was not satisfied with praising God for all the riches God had so graciously provided. Instead, he used those blessings for his glory. As a result, Satan lost his position. Don't take credit when the credit belongs to God. There is nothing that you are, nothing that you have, or anything that you do, which God did not give to you. Give credit where credit is due.

Prayer: Lord, forgive me when I take credit for good work when all the credit belongs to you. May I give you the glory for every good thing in my life. Any good in me is because of who I am in you. All praise and honor are yours, Lord God Almighty. Amen.

Scripture for further reading: 2 Corinthians 8:13–15; Proverbs 26:12; Psalm 50:23; 1 Peter 4:11.

_____

_____

_____

_____

_____

_____

_____

Glory

Do you know anyone so full of themselves that they are miserable to be around? Do you know anyone at work who takes credit for others' ideas? That's how God must feel when we brag, "This is what I accomplished." Remember, every gift, talent, and success are from God. Give God the glory. First Corinthians 10:31 says, "Whatever you do, do it all for the glory of God."

Prayer: Lord, thank you for providing every talent and opportunity. You are the source of every jaw-dropping, mind-blowing, and heart-racing thing in my life, and there are many. Help me to overcome pride and arrogance. Remind me that it is only by your grace that I receive every blessing. Amen.

Scripture for further reading: Jeremiah 31:35; Malachi 2:2; Genesis 11:31–32.

Let It Shine

Remember the song, "This little light of mine; I'm going to let it shine; this little light of mine, I'm going to let it shine. Let it shine. Let it shine. Let it shine." Harry Dixon Loes wrote this childhood hymn in the 1920s. Do you wonder what light the song is referring to? The light is all the love, joy, kindness, and gentleness that reflects God's glory. Matthew 5:16 says, "Let your light shine before men, that they may see your good deeds and glorify your Father in heaven."

Prayer: Lord, your glorious light is within me. Help me to sparkle. Help me to shimmer and shine. As a child of light, I pray to resonate with the love, joy, victory, and success available each day in Christ Jesus. Your glory is alive in me. I rejoice in you always. Amen.

Scripture for further reading: John 8:12; Ephesians 5:8; Daniel 1:23; Matthew 5:14–16; Philippians 4:4.

Success

Say this prayer every day, "Jesus, come into my life." With this prayer, you are inviting the power available through grace to be present in you for each day. You are invoking His presence, grace, goodness, and glory in your life. We can, with confidence, commit to the Lord whatever we do, knowing that it will succeed. "Jesus said, 'Let the little children come to me, and do not hinder them, for the kingdom of heaven belongs to such as these'" (Matthew 19:14).

Prayer: Jesus, your presence in me is my hope for glory. Live in me and through me. Jesus, light the TNT within me to cause your beauty to explode, empower, and enlarge my life. Amen.

Scripture for further reading: Proverbs 16:3; Ephesians 3:14; 2 Corinthians 4:6–7; 2 Corinthians 13:5.

_____

_____

_____

_____

_____

_____

_____

_____

_____

Non-Negotiable Qualities

Choosing a partner in business or life can bring happiness or heartache. Think about the qualities that are important to you in selecting companions:

- Are they virtuous? Do they demonstrate honesty, responsibility, trust, respect, and humility?
- Are they loving? Will they be supportive, affectionate, faithful, generous, and loyal?
- Are they Christian? What is their faith? Do they serve God or themselves?
- How do they communicate? Are they articulate, loud, quiet, verbal, or non-verbal?
- How do they handle money? Are they a spender, hoarder, generous, or a good steward?
- What are their friends and family like, and how do they treat them?
- How do they act in different circumstances?
- What happens when you say "no?"

Scripture shows that character matters: "Now Daniel so distinguished himself among the administrators and the satraps by his exceptional qualities that the king planned to set him over the whole kingdom" (Daniel 6:3).

Prayer: Lord, help me to seek godly relations and aspire to those qualities that are pleasing to you. Amen.

Scripture for further reading: Hebrews 13:7; 1 Timothy 3:2; 1 Titus 7–14.

Do It Today

Why wait until tomorrow when you can do it today? Whenever you set out to do something, whether great or small, whether afraid or excited, always acknowledge God first, and then take action. James 2:17 says, "faith by itself, if it is not accompanied by action, is dead." The first step is always the hardest, so recognize that taking even a small step toward your goal can produce significant results. Jesus doesn't want someone else to take care of whatever He has prepared for you to accomplish. If you turn and run from the task, you'll eventually face it again. When you take a step in the right direction, it will help you gather momentum. Do your best so that you'll never be ashamed. Go. Be a doer of the word, and not only a hearer.

Prayer: Lord, I know I can do all things through you. This confidence alone ignites faith in me to move forward to accomplish all that you set before me. Amen.

Scripture for further reading: 2 Corinthians 10:7–11; 2 Timothy 2:15; John 15:16; James 1:22.

_____

_____

_____

_____

_____

_____

_____

You've Got the Power

When the world seems overwhelming, say this prayer, "Lord, help me be strong in you. First John 5:4–5 says, "For everyone born of God overcomes the world... Who is it that overcomes the world? Only the one who believes that Jesus is the Son of God." If you dwell on a problem, it gives power to the problem. Instead, focus on the promises of God. Focus on the power and authority you possess over the schemes of the enemy. Here is an effective method of taking control over the problem: turn your palms down while releasing your pain, sorrow, or confusion to God. Then turn your palms up, praying to receive power from God to restore joy, success, and confidence. Take back the freedom that comes by taking it to the Lord. You've got the power.

Prayer: Lord, you are my fortress. I put my trust in you. Be with me now and with my loved ones. Let us experience your presence today and know the power and authority you have placed within us. In Jesus' precious name. Amen.

Scripture for further reading: Hebrews 4:9–11; Ephesians 3:8–12; Ephesians 6:10–12; Psalm 1:1–3.

_____

_____

_____

_____

_____

_____

Struggles

Do you wonder about life struggles? Many people falsely believe that a just and fair God wants all good people to prosper and all bad people to suffer. First Peter 1:6 and 5:10 remind us that suffering is temporary. It's helpful to remember that struggle serves to develop our greatest strengths. Most people spend more time and energy focused on problems than on keeping the faith to find solutions. Struggles serve to strengthen our faith and bring future reward.

Prayer: Lord, when trials come, help me to take ten. Rather than dwell on the problem, help me to think of the immeasurable blessings of the moment. One of which will be to tell the devil, "Oh, thank you for reminding me to give my problems to God. He's on the throne. He'll take care of it." Then I can go on and do what you want me to do, Lord. I can move forward to laugh, enjoy your goodness, count blessings, receive favor, and celebrate life. Lord, increase my faith. Faith has greater worth than gold. Amen.

Scripture for further reading: Psalm 66:10–12; Malachi 3:3; Job 23:10; Proverbs 17:3.

Let's Walk Through This Together

"A great door for effective work has opened to me, and there are many who oppose me" (1 Corinthians 16:9). This scripture refers to Satan's hope to keep you from fulfilling your destiny. He knows that you will become a powerful force for God. So, understand that the going will not always be easy. Fulfilling your future calling is going to take effort and determination. Never give up. Don't complain and give the devil a foothold. Get rid of negative thoughts that hold you captive. There's a saying, "Keep on keeping on." Just keep walking with God until you see His full will come to pass in your life.

Prayer: Oh, Lord, I know the devil won't roll out the red carpet for me to do your will. The enemy fights me the hardest when he knows I'm moving toward victory. I pray to make the devil tremble whenever my feet hit the floor in the morning, knowing I am an on-fire, powerful force to do God's work. I need you every hour Lord. Help me cling to the triumph of life accessed through your power, wisdom, and victory. I pray this in the mighty name of Jesus. Amen.

Scripture for further reading: 1 Corinthians 16:9; 2 Corinthians 8:10–12; Joshua 1:9; Deuteronomy 3:18.

_____

_____

_____

_____

I Can Do This

Do you wonder what your purpose is on this earth? Do you think about what you can offer the world? Help others triumph over challenges that you've already faced and conquered. Overcoming, and sharing your experience in the struggle, is your calling. In 1 Thessalonians 2:9, Paul tells us, "Surely you remember, brothers and sisters, our toil and hardship; we worked night and day in order not to be a burden to anyone while we preached the gospel of God to you." Whatever your vocation, do it with zeal. Do it to the best of your ability. Show the love, goodness, and kindness of God.

Prayer: Father, God, help me to realize my specific purpose. It is incredible to think that you, the Creator of the universe, trust me to do something so special that only I can do it through you. I can't do it on my own. I'll mess it up. But when I partner with you and remain in you and you in me, I can finish the job successfully. Thank you for trusting me and using me to accomplish your work. Amen.

Scripture for further reading: 2 Corinthians 7:5–10; Ephesians 2:10; Ephesians 3:12; Proverbs 22:6; Matthew 28:19.

_____

_____

_____

_____

_____

_____

Your Choice: Good, Better, Best

What does your life reflect? Are you perfect? Probably not. We all have imperfections. Think about your response to life's challenges. Your reaction to problems can be eye-opening. There are three choices in response. The first option is to find blame or dwell in despair; this is not a good choice. It doesn't solve the problem or make you feel better. Second, stuffing the situation and moving forward is a minimally better solution, but you and the problem remain miserable. The best solution is to deal with your mistakes, issues, and pain. Learn how to use life challenges for good, and grow while helping others along the way. Isaiah 61:3 reminds us to run forward toward the best life God wants for us. "Provide for those who grieve in Zion — to bestow on them a crown of beauty instead of ashes, the oil of joy instead of mourning, and a garment of praise instead of a spirit of despair. They will be called oaks of righteousness, a planting of the Lord for the display of His splendor."

Prayer: Father God, give me the oil of joy for mourning and the garment of praise for the spirit of heaviness. Worship is a gift, and your will. Help me face obstacles that hold me back from the glorious life you planned for me. Help me to lean on you and seek godly counsel. You created us for connectedness; to grow in you and with those, you bring in our lives. Thank you, Lord Jesus, Amen.

Scripture for further reading: Philippians 3:17–21; 2 Thessalonians 2:15–16; 1 Timothy 1:18–20.

Best Practice

How do you deal with pain? God wants you to get past the pain and share your experience with others. What mistakes did you make? How did you feel? How did you get through it? How did God help you in your weakness? Your testimony will strengthen others, give them hope, and lead them to Christ. "The accuser of our brothers and sisters, who accuses them before our God day and night, has been hurled down. They triumphed over him by the blood of the Lamb and by the word of their testimony" (Revelations 12:10–11). Share your testimony and help others to heal. Here's how to move forward in victory:

- Write down every detail of what happened.
- Write down how your experience hurt you, how it made you feel.
- What helped you get through it?
- What did you gain through the process? What did you learn? Are you stronger, wiser, more courageous, brave, or loving? God wouldn't allow it to happen if there was not something to gain.
- Encourage others who need to hear your testimony.

Prayer: Lord, I know that any pain and suffering I endure will lead to good; this is your promise for those who know and love you. But it is so hard to see or understand at the time. Help me to experience you during these times and persevere. Guide me to use the wisdom to help someone else. I pray this in Jesus' name. Amen.

Scripture for further reading: 2 Thessalonians 1:3–12; 1 Peter 2:19; 1 Peter 4:12–19; Hebrews 12:1–11.

Prayer for the Mission

What is your mission in this world? First Peter 3:15 says, "But in your hearts revere Christ as Lord. Always be prepared to give an answer to everyone who asks you to give the reason for the hope that you have. But do this with gentleness and respect." Pray for wisdom and revelation. Pray that your heart is open to the hope of riches in His glorious inheritance and available through His remarkable power. Prayer is an essential tool for your mission.

Prayer: Father, help me to know you better and show others your love and grace. Help me to become a fisher of men. Thank you for the privilege of prayer. I pray in Jesus' name, the name above all names. Amen.

Scripture for further reading: 1 Corinthians 7:3–5; Jeremiah 10:23; Romans 1:8–12; Ephesians 1:15–23.

_____

_____

_____

_____

_____

_____

_____

_____

_____

Excellence

You are a child of an excellent God. God is just, faithful, and upright, and this seed of excellence is within you. Excellent people reach higher, try longer, and work harder. Titus 3:8 says, "This is a trustworthy saying. And I want you to stress these things, so that those who have trusted in God may be careful to devote themselves to doing what is good. These things are excellent and profitable for everyone."

Prayer: Lord, I've given presents to people who never use them. I try to imagine how you must feel, giving us gifts of beauty, music, generosity, encouragement, and taking them all for granted. Everything that I am is a gift from you. You are delighted when I use these gifts for your glory. Help me, Lord, to recognize, appreciate, and use these gifts to glorify you. Amen.

Scripture for further reading: Deuteronomy 32:4; Deuteronomy 12:28; 1 Corinthians 8:1–7; 1 Corinthians 7:7.

Get It All

Mediocre people are happy with being average, and that's what they get. People who complain there's not enough time to achieve what they want may not have their priorities straight. The highest priority is to use your time wisely and pursue excellence. A person of distinction may not get everything they want all at once, but they can manage to get it all over time. Proverbs 31:31 talks about the person of excellence, who manages to get it all: "Honor her for all that her hands have done, and let her works bring her praise at the city gate."

Prayer: God, I want everything I do to be praiseworthy. It takes time and effort to be excellent. With your help, I pray that the habit of excellence becomes second nature to me; make it a part of my being. Amen.

Scripture for further reading: 1 Corinthians 12:31–13:3; 1 Timothy 3:13; Romans 2:5–11.

Laziness

There's a German proverb that says, "Tomorrow, tomorrow, not today. That's what all the lazy people say." Lazy people reach for nothing, and they get nothing for their reward. Put forth the effort to maximize your potential. You will win the admiration of others and gain confidence in yourself. Ezekiel 29:20 says, "I have given him Egypt as a reward for his efforts because he and his army did it for me, declares the Sovereign Lord."

Prayer: Father, I thank you for the blessing of this wisdom — to work to maximize my potential. Thank you for the energy and this day to pursue it. Please keep this knowledge fresh within me each day. Amen.

Scripture for further reading: Ezekiel 29:20; 2 Peter 1:10–11; Hebrews 6:10–11; Romans 2:5–11.

Integrity

Who is someone with integrity? It is someone with a trustworthy soul, too caring to judge, too thoughtful to gossip, and has a heart after God. Proverbs 13:6 says, "Righteousness guards the person of integrity."

Prayer: Lord, the Bible tells me that you love me so much, you sent your only Son to die for my sins. I am made righteous, not by what I do, but by the blood of Jesus. I will not deny my integrity. I am made righteous in Christ through faith. Help me to keep a clean conscience and maintain innocence. Give me an upright heart and mind so that I may walk with integrity. Amen.

Scripture for further reading: Psalm 7:8–10; Romans 3:21–26; Job 27:5–6.

_____

_____

_____

_____

_____

_____

_____

_____

What's on Your Mind?

Think about what you're thinking about. Right now, what is most prominent on your mind? Is it pure, kind, holy, patient, loving, and acceptable to God? First Corinthians 13:11 says, "When I was a child I talked like a child, I thought like a child, I reasoned like a child. When I became a man, I put the ways of childhood behind me."

Prayer: Lord, I confess that my thoughts are selfish, prideful, and unloving. I think a lot about what makes me happy. Forgive me for being selfish; change me. My goal is to focus on things that are eternal and pleasing to you. I ask for your grace to keep my mind, heart, and soul growing in this wisdom. Amen.

Scripture for further reading: 2 Corinthians 10:3–5; Lamentations 3:21–25; 2 Peter 3:14–18.

_____

_____

_____

_____

_____

_____

_____

_____

_____

Spur One Another

Ever wonder why some people are so mean-spirited? Hurting people hurt people. Instead of thinking about how that person needs to change, think about what they've accomplished despite their hurts. Hebrews 10:24 reminds us to, "let us consider how we may spur one another on toward love and good deeds."

Prayer: Lord, as I read the message today, I think about a loved one who is difficult. To let off steam, I find myself talking negatively about them. Instead of gossiping or venting to anyone who'll hear me, help me to realize how I can encourage them, instead. Helping others to remember happier times, find inspiration, and make good memories, all serve to refresh the soul. Sharing a smile can also fill others with joy and encourages them to respond likewise. Thank you for your wisdom, Lord Jesus. Amen.

Scripture for further reading: 2 Corinthians 9:1–3; Romans 9:1–5; Romans 5:6–11.

Make It a Brighter Day

It takes just as much time and energy to be kind as it does to be rude. So why aren't people more thoughtful? When you run into someone less than considerate, here's what you can do: you can be kinder. Consider why they're like that. It is easier to understand their demeanor when you find out a little more about them and what made them that way. It doesn't excuse their behavior. Being more thoughtful keeps the devil from getting a foothold and allowing others' lousy behavior to ruin your day. Ephesians 5:21 reminds us to "submit to one another out of reverence for Christ." Make it a brighter day.

Prayer: Lord, I want to learn to be more thoughtful. My mother used to tell me, "Don't judge someone until you've walked in their shoes." Well, I don't want to judge anyone, because that dishonors you. Besides, there's still much for them to learn on this journey called life, just as there is for me. Help me to understand what others are going through so that I can take steps to make it a brighter day. Amen.

Scripture for further reading: Philippians 4:14–16; Colossians 2:16–19; Ephesians 4:27.

Procrastination

Tick Tock. Are you killing time? There is a Chinese proverb that says the best time to plant a tree was twenty years ago. The next best time is now. Procrastination is a very deceptive tool of the devil. If you put things off, it creates more stress later. Ecclesiastes 5:4, says, "When you make a vow to God, do not delay to fulfill it. He has no pleasure in fools; fulfill your vow."

Prayer: Lord, I don't want to be foolish by putting things off. Give me the energy and motivation to get things done expediently. Help me to complete the task. Amen.

Scripture for further reading: 1 Corinthians 14:40; Ecclesiastes 11:40; Proverbs 10:4; James 4:17.

_____

_____

_____

_____

_____

_____

_____

_____

_____

_____

Blessed With What I Need

God supplies every need according to the riches of His glory. God wants you to be prosperous. Don't believe it? Deuteronomy 28:9–11 says, "if you keep the commands of the Lord your God and walk in obedience to Him…the Lord will grant you abundant Prosperity." If you diligently seek Him, He will bring you rewards now and into eternity.

Prayer: Lord, direct me to invest my time, money, and energy into matters of the heart. Steer me away from putting a value on temporal things of this world. You provide all that I need. My job is not to build an empire, but to serve you and the kingdom. Help me devote my time, money, and energy to what is everlasting. Kingdom living is real prosperity. I know that committing to a life of status and carefree luxury, on the other hand, is idolatry. Amen.

Scripture for further reading: 2 Corinthians 9:8; Luke 6:38; Philippians 4:19.

_____

_____

_____

_____

_____

_____

_____

_____

Guidance

Do you trust God for guidance? Many people get frustrated and struggle because they try to be their own captain on this journey called life. But God promises that He will guide us and direct our paths if we seek and trust in Him. Proverbs 3:5–6 says, "Trust in the Lord with all your heart and lean not on your own understanding; in all your ways submit to Him, and he will make your paths straight."

Prayer: Lord, help me to understand how to make the best use of my time and follow your will. I need your guidance in every choice I make. I trust that you will lead me, as I seek you. Amen.

Scripture for further reading: Galatians 2:14–19; Ephesians 5:15–17; John 9:4.

Led by God

I don't have all the answers. When I try to do things on my own, I often make a mess of them. Jeremiah 33:3 says, "Call to me and I will answer you and tell you great and unsearchable things you do not know." Have you been confident about handling a situation only to find out that it backfired? Many times, what worked in the past won't apply to similar circumstances. Time, people, and conditions are different. We discover that relying on our understanding is not enough. It's a reminder that God has more for us to learn. It's a reminder to lean on God. It's a reminder to be led by God.

Prayer: Lord, I know that any confusion or doubt will give way to a new understanding when I seek you. Your grace fills every lack in me. You take my hand and lead me. I thank you for your abundant wisdom and guidance. You provide everything I need to succeed. There is so much that I am thankful for. Amen.

Scripture for further reading: Galatians 1:10–11; 1 John 2:1; Proverbs 28:13; Proverbs 37:24; Romans 3:23.

_____

_____

_____

_____

_____

_____

Persistence

Some of the greatest heroes are those who suffer from learning disabilities. They are heroes because they never give up. They learn, sometimes the hard way, that persistence pays off. They get the help they need and keep moving forward. Step by step, they make progress. Romans 2:6 says, "God will repay each person according to what they have done." Persistence pays off.

Prayer: Father, give me the gift of persistence. When challenges come, help me stay encouraged to keep trying again and again, and with greater conviction and resolve. Amen.

Scripture for further reading: Luke 21:19; Hebrews 6:11; James 1:12.

I Know I Can

Remember that story about *"The Little Engine That Could,"* written by Watty Piper? The little engine keeps a positive attitude and stays focused on getting ahead. The little engine keeps repeating, "I think I can; I think I can." When challenges seem insurmountable, tell yourself, "With God, I know I can. I know I can." Second Timothy 3:16–17 tells us, "All Scripture is God-breathed and is useful for teaching, rebuking, correcting, and training in righteousness, so that the servant of God may be thoroughly equipped for every good work."

Prayer: Lord, you are my strength and my shield. I ask for zeal to stride forward with renewed vigor for the challenges of today. Lord, help me stay on track, knowing I am up for any challenge, for you are with me. Amen.

Scripture for further reading: 2 Corinthians 9:2; 1 Timothy 6:20; 1 Corinthians 15:58; Romans 12:11.

_____

_____

_____

_____

_____

_____

_____

_____

Get the Job Done

Try, try, and try again. Don't give up. Get the job done. You will gain many life rewards by learning to plug away until the very end. To succeed, you need tenacity. To persevere through ups and downs, never give up. Hebrews 12:1 says, "Let us throw off everything that hinders and the sin that so easily entangles. And let us run with perseverance, the race marked out for us." No matter what, be resolved, endure to the end, and get the job done.

Prayer: God, I thank you for everything I need to persevere. In you, I have the courage, strength, and endurance to get the job done. In you, I have the wisdom to remove obstacles and find resources to be successful. My confidence and victory come from you. Amen.

Scripture for further reading: Ecclesiastes 7:8; 2 Corinthians 8:10–12; John 4:34; Matthew 25:23.

Sharing

For many, the world is dark, cold, and full of despair. Your flame burns so brightly, why not share your love and warmth with others. Let others see how the love of God has changed your life. "To the weak I became weak, to win the weak. I have become all things to all people so that by all possible means I might save some. I do all this for the sake of the gospel, that I may share in its blessings" (1 Corinthians 9:22–23). What a privilege it is to witness what the Word of God will accomplish.

Prayer: Lord, may I share the light of your love with those who need compassion, kindness, love, and joy. May the knowledge of the gospel spread rapidly so that more people will know God's love and experience the comfort and abundance of a changed life with you. May I be a flame that sparks warmth in this cold, dark world because of your amazing love. Amen.

Scripture for further reading: 2 Thessalonians 3:1–5; 1 Timothy 1:13–14; Colossians 1:28.

What's Your Secret?

There are so many hearts that are hardened and will not accept the good news of Jesus Christ. God desires that no one is lost. If you knew the secret to cure cancer, wouldn't you want to tell someone? How much more critical the secret to eternal life. Helping a single soul gain eternal salvation is more important than anything else you will do in life. Nonbelievers are often very defensive about hearing a sermon. So, how can you tell others the good news? You can help to soften their hearts. Pray for them, love them, spend time with them, and then, you will be able to share the gospel. God will do the rest. Isaiah 55:10–11 says, "As the rain and snow come down from the heavens and do not return to it without watering the earth and making it bud and flourish, so that it yields seed for the sower and bread for the eater, so is my word that goes out from my mouth: It will not return to me empty."

Prayer: Lord, please use me to spread the good news of your faithfulness. May the eyes and hearts of all those in my life be opened to hear your word. Water the word so that it will grow within them and give them hope, love, and a bright future. Amen.

Scripture for further reading: Romans 10:14–15; Romans 11:25–32; Philippians 4:18–19.

_____

_____

_____

_____

_____

Blessings

What you say is what you get. If you speak of blessings, that's what you'll receive. If you curse life, that too, is what you'll get. Words are powerful instruments that create your reality. What comes out of your mouth? Is it pure and positive, or is it evil and negative? It is written in Psalm 17:3, "Though you probe my heart, though you examine me at night and test me, you will find that I have planned no evil; my mouth has not transgressed." Your life will reflect what you say.

Prayer: Lord, I know that words are power. Help me only to speak blessings. I profess grace over my loved ones now, Lord, that their lives are full and radiant because of the wisdom and joy they receive through you. I speak peace over our nations and knowledge for all leaders. I pray comfort for those in need and guidance for those who are lost. I pray victory for everyone who hears your word and receives it. Thank you, Lord, for victory in the power of your name. Amen.

Scripture for further reading: James 3:10; Luke 1:42; Proverbs 11:11.

_____

_____

_____

_____

_____

_____

_____

It Just Takes a Second

Every second of every day has infinite value. Take a moment to open the door for a disabled woman. Five precious minutes, holding a child can never be replaced. Console a friend for twenty minutes. Celebrate your child's birthday, all day. Take a week to enjoy the beach with family. Life is so short. Every day, look for the blessing, and be a blessing. Proverbs 11:25 says, "A generous person will prosper; whoever refreshes others will be refreshed." Be a blessing to others, and your life will be abundantly blessed.

Prayer: Lord, help me find the blessings of the day. You've provided so many; I don't want to miss one of them. Missing the glory of a happy day is waste. Don't miss the laughter of children playing in the leaves. I don't want to miss the smile on a loved one's face or overlook a friend's joy and celebration. Help me live each day to the fullest, being a blessing, and being blessed. Help me name each benefit, one by one. Thank you, Lord Jesus, for this glorious day. Amen.

Scripture for further reading: Hebrews 13:16; 2 Corinthians 9:12–15; Zechariah 8:13.

School of Hard Knocks

Why does God allow bad things to happen? We discover more about our character and what we're made of when life throws a curveball. Through struggles and storms, we learn patience, prayer, trust, and faith in God. Difficult times occur so that we can learn something we'll need another day. If we don't learn the first time, we'll have to take that test again. Once we learn the lesson, we can help others who are having similar issues. Romans 2:6 says, "God will repay each person according to what they have done." Find the lesson in each challenge.

Prayer: Lord, I pray to be an astute learner. I pray not to continually learn things the hard way. Instead of learning through hard knocks, give me a teachable heart. May I always be receptive to your Word. Give me the heart to learn spiritual truth and godly wisdom. Amen.

Scripture for further reading: 1 Corinthians 2:13–14; 1 Corinthians 4:16–18; Proverbs 12:1; Proverbs 13:18; James 1:1–27.

Sexuality

Sex was God's idea. Sex is the divine consecrated connection between a husband and wife. When we align our lives with this spiritual truth, it leads to deeper relations. Walking in this kind of intimacy, unobstructed by impurity, we attract all the joy available through God's infinite love. If we choose to keep sex pure and sacred, we activate increased probability for further spiritual and miraculous good. Pure and perfect love has the power to make all things right. In purity, we attract positive energy. Your body is an extraordinary living, breathing reflection of love. Don't let circumstances tempt you to deviate or compromise from God's plan. First Corinthians 6:18–20 says, "Flee from sexual immorality. All other sins a person commits are outside the body, but whoever sins sexually, sins against their own body.... Therefore, honor God with your bodies."

Prayer: Father, give me the wisdom to regard sexuality as sacred, and experience it in the way that you designed it. Help me to honor you by being mindful of how I use this gift. Amen.

Scripture for further reading: Galatians 5:19–25; Ephesians 5:3–7; Ephesians 5:21–33.

_____

_____

_____

_____

_____

_____

Mind, Body, and Soul

Marriage should be monogamous but never monotonous. God expects that both husband and wife should be satisfied in holy splendor. God interwove the mind, body, and soul. Whatever touches one aspect of our being, has a bearing on the others. Both husband and wife are responsible for ensuring total satisfaction in marital happiness, fulfilling love, and pleasurable sex. Both should exalt one another in public. Both should be intentional to keep from annoying or frustrating the other. Both should present themselves worthy of affection. Proverbs 11:22 says, "Like a gold ring in a pig's snout is a beautiful woman who shows no discretion."

Prayer: Lord, in our marriage, may we be a source of constant delight for one another. Teach us discretion. Give us wisdom and discipline in how we present ourselves. May we treat one another as a prize, worthy of love and affection. May we promote one another in front of others. Give us each a pure and gentle love that grows in devotion. Amen.

Scripture for further reading: Proverbs 5:19; 1 Timothy 2:9–10; Romans 3:19–20; Romans 6:11–14; Romans 19:23.

Naked and Unashamed

Enjoy sex. Make the same choices about sexual relations that you would other areas of life. Have sex, according to God's plan. Sex apart from what God intended injures the spirit, destroys marriage, promotes promiscuousness, and abuse abounds. Sex outside of marriage can have innumerable, long-lasting, and painful consequences. Sex, according to God's plan, nourishes the spirit, improves marital relations, and promotes family generations to celebrate. Sex in the marriage is fulfilling and is a celebration of a time when "Adam and his wife were both naked, and they felt no shame" (Genesis 2:25). Such sex honors God.

Prayer: Dear Father, help me to respect my body as your temple, and keep sexual relations pure and holy. Amen.

Scripture for further reading: Ephesians 5:29; Job 12:3; Psalm 139:13–14; 1 Corinthians 3:16–27; 1 Corinthians 6:12–20.

What a Fool

Too often, we underestimate the power of listening. The word silent has the same letters as the word listen. Be silent and listen. Time spent listening is well invested. When we're talking, we repeat what we already know. But when we listen, there's a chance to learn something new. One of the highest forms of love is listening. Sometimes people don't need to get advice; they just need to feel heard. Be quiet until you know others feel heard. Sometimes people just need someone to understand. Be silent with a heart to understand. Proverbs 18:13 says, "To answer before listening — that is folly and shame." Whoever listens is wise.

Prayer: Lord, I pray to listen more than I talk. By listening more and speaking less, I can fully reflect on what is being said, before spouting off an undesired, irrelevant, or flagrant opinion. In listening more and talking less, I might gain wisdom and appear less a fool. I pray for wisdom in this area. Amen.

Scripture for further reading: Galatians 6:1; Proverbs 2:2; Proverbs 17:28; Proverbs 18:2; 1 John 5:14.

_____

_____

_____

_____

_____

_____

Leadership

Thoughtfulness is a characteristic of great leaders. People are willing to work harder and sacrifice more for leaders who are sensitive to others' hearts. Thoughtful leaders are held in high esteem because they recognize, gain insight, develop, and celebrate each person's calling. Thoughtful leaders respond, restore, correct, and challenge others. Philippians 2:3 says, "Do nothing out of selfish ambition or vain conceit. Rather, in humility value others above yourselves."

Prayer: God, help me to gain leadership skills that Jesus portrayed throughout the Bible. Amen.

Scripture for further reading: Galatians 6:2–6; Romans 12:6–8; Philippians 2:1–9.

_____

_____

_____

_____

_____

_____

_____

_____

_____

Finding the Love of Your Life

I'd been praying a long time to meet the love of my life. But, one morning, I prayed vehemently, "Hear my prayer, God. Bring me the love of my life. Everyone I've met so far, both you and I know, are not right for me. Won't you please bring me the love of my life today?" Now, I don't usually make such bold requests, and God doesn't often answer my prayers so quickly, but later that day, when I met that tall Texan, I knew. I prayed, "God, thank you for answering my prayer. Thank you." Three months later, we were married. God will lead you to the love of your life. He brings the right person when you first acknowledge God. Then He will direct your path. Colossians 3:17 says, "And whatever you do, in word or deed, do everything in the name of the Lord Jesus, giving thanks to God the Father through Him." God will reward you when you do. Wait on God's timing to find that perfect person.

Prayer: Lord, I put my faith and trust in you for all things. Thank you for helping me to wait for your timing in bringing the right person, at the right time, and to live, love, and laugh with. Amen.

Scripture for further reading: Song of Songs 2:7; Genesis 2:18; Proverbs 19:2; Ruth 1:16–17.

Worth the Wait

Why is it essential to wait on God's timing to find your partner for life? Suppose you want to buy a car, but you only have $2,000. You're not going to buy much for $2,000. But if you wait, you'll have time to save money, plan better, and consider all your options. It's the same with finding the love of your life. If you don't wait to have a serious relationship with someone, then you only know the "dating" person who is on their best behavior. Waiting gives you time to test whether your attraction is love or lust. Waiting allows your relationship to withstand the test of time. "Love is patient; love is kind. It does not envy; it does not boast; it is not proud. It does not dishonor others; it is not self-seeking; it is not easily angered; it keeps no record of wrongs. Love does not delight in evil but rejoices with the truth. It always protects, always trusts, always hopes, always perseveres. Love never fails" (1 Corinthians 13:4–8). You are a child of God, the King of kings. Make sure you don't marry a frog. Waiting allows you to learn if that special someone is truly a prince or princess.

Prayer: Lord, thank you for this lesson. I pray that my loved ones and I appreciate and practice the wisdom in waiting, not only in relationships but in all our endeavors. In Jesus' name, I pray. Amen.

Scripture for further reading: Romans 12:1–2; Romans 13:13; Romans 15:5–6; Philippians 2:1–2.

_____

_____

_____

_____

_____

Lust

Don't give in to lust. Romans 1:25–29 says, "They exchanged the truth of God for a lie and worshiped and served created things... Because of this, God gave them over to shameful lusts. Even their women exchanged natural relations for unnatural ones. In the same way, the men also abandoned natural relations with women and were inflamed with lust for one another." Don't lust after things that are not of God; in fact, don't desire anything more than you want an intimate relationship with Him. We serve a jealous God. Nothing should come before Him. Seek first to be in His presence and worship Him alone.

Prayer: Lord, lust can be a love of many things. It refers to physical and sexual attraction and power, money, success, prestige, reputation, or possessions. Help me, Lord, to place you ahead of everything else in my life. Amen.

Scripture for further reading: Psalm 101:3; 1 John 2:16; Romans 8:6.

Self-Worth

Don't base your self-worth on someone else's opinion. Don't base your self-worth on how others treat you. Your self-esteem should come from God alone. You are a child of God and loved by the one who counts the most. God has given you capabilities, resources, and a life of your own. He has given you everything you need to live a happy, successful life. When you maximize your God-given gifts, you will realize that you are a person of worth, not of weight. "Rather, it should be that of your inner self, the unfading beauty of a gentle and quiet spirit, which is of great worth in God's sight" (1 Peter 3:4).

Prayer: Lord, help me to realize my value and self-worth. My worth depends solely on who I am in you. I am the child of the King of the universe. You give me gifts, talents, and abilities to do what only I am prepared to do. No one else is so fully equipped to accomplish what God has so thoughtfully designed just for me to complete. What a blessing beyond measure. Amen.

Scripture for further reading: Ephesians 2:10; 1 Peter 4:10–11; Matthew 5:14–16.

Laughter Is Good Medicine

God designed your body with natural pain killers called endorphins. They are released when you laugh. God made endorphins to improve your health and happiness. According to Psalm 126:2, laughter is good medicine: "Our mouths were filled with laughter, our tongues with songs of joy....The Lord has done great things." Laugh often.

Prayer: Lord, help me to find something to laugh about every day. There is too much joy to miss. I will make a purposeful effort to find, share, and experience joy and laughter. Thank you, Lord Jesus. Amen.

Scripture for further reading: Genesis 21:6; Job 8:21; Psalm 126:2.

_____

_____

_____

_____

_____

_____

_____

_____

_____

_____

_____

Truthfulness

The mind is the devil's playground. The devil can easily lead brilliant people away from the truth of Christ. People with firm convictions can be very persuasive. Don't allow anyone or anything to sway you away from the truth of God. Pray and affirm God's presence within you and say publicly, what is true. In Proverbs 12:22, it says, "The Lord detests lying lips, but He delights in people who are trustworthy."

Prayer: Father, thank you that I serve a God of truth. Help me to seek, speak, and discern what is right. Amen.

Scripture for further reading: 1 Timothy 1:1–12; John 17:17.

_____

_____

_____

_____

_____

_____

_____

_____

_____

_____

_____

No Time Like the Present

How can you resist temptation and choose to do right? Stand up for what you believe. Speak up when you see people making the wrong choices. Step out against things that you know are wrong. Romans 12:2 instructs us, "Do not conform to the pattern of this world, but be transformed by the renewing of your mind. Then you will be able to test and approve what God's will is; His good, pleasing, and perfect will."

Prayer: Teach me, Lord, and refresh my faith. I ask for grace and courage to begin fresh and full of life today. Teach me to hear your voice. There's never a more perfect time than the present, to step out and choose to do right. Amen.

Scripture for further reading: 2 Corinthians 7:1–4; Galatians 2:1–4; Deuteronomy 30:15–19.

Power and Authority Are Mine

Do you get impatient with family members? Has a friend ever said or done something to cause you to lose it? The enemy knows how to push your buttons, and he uses loved ones to make you angry and impatient. The devil knows that if you lose peace, you lose the blessings that God has prepared for you. The enemy hates you and is jealous of the love God has for you. The devil will do everything within his power to stop the flow of blessings in your life. Well, you've got the final say. God gave you power and authority over the enemy. Refuse to take offense; choose instead to walk in peace and love. Don't let the devil win. What is your choice in how to respond? Choose to show patience and respect. Even though it may be difficult, this sacrifice will produce spectacular rewards. Luke 11:28 reminds us, "Blessed rather are those who hear the word of God and obey it."

Prayer: Father Almighty, help me to be patient, especially with mean people. Help me demonstrate a higher level of self-discipline and obedience. I know it pleases you and will produce great blessings when I do. Amen.

Scripture for further reading: Ephesians 5:14–20; Romans 12: 17–21; Colossians 1:9–10.

Temptations

How many times are you tempted to compromise, or do something you know isn't right? When tempted, don't do something you know is wrong. Ephesians 6:17 reminds us, "Take the helmet of salvation and the sword of the Spirit, which is the Word of God." Every time Jesus was tempted by the devil, He responded with Scripture. Jesus quoted three verses when the devil tempted him for forty days. Memorize Scripture to overcome temptation. There is power in God's Word, and Satan fears it.

Prayer: Lord, help me to learn Scripture so that I will be armed with spiritual bullets to fight against the devil's attacks. In Jesus' name, I pray. Amen.

Scripture for further reading: Romans 8:5–8; Hebrews 2:17–18; Deuteronomy 6:13–16; Deuteronomy 8:3.

_____

_____

_____

_____

_____

_____

_____

_____

_____

Whom Should I Serve?

You can't serve both God and money. Followers of Christ make Him their priority, place their confidence in Him, and worship Him only. Lovers of money place their trust in possessions. Money becomes their idol of worship. Money worshipers seek first, more money. "No one can serve two masters. Either you will hate the one and love the other, or you will be devoted to the one and despise the other. You cannot serve both God and money" (Matthew 6:24). If you live to make more money, you are not living to serve God. If you live to serve God, God will take care of your needs.

Prayer: Lord, help me seek you with all my mind, heart, and soul. I seek you with every fiber of my being. Be on the throne of my life forever. Amen.

Scripture for further reading: Philippians 1:19–26; Philippians 3:9–11; Romans 6:8–10.

A Life Full of Stuff

There is more to life than having more stuff. Do you go through withdrawal pains if you don't buy a new pair of shoes every week? Does it make you feel sick when you can't buy all the movies you want? Do you get the shakes when your friends drive cars that you can't afford? Well, stop. You will probably get dizzy spells when you force yourself to stop buying, buying, buying. But remind yourself you are going through a serious transition. Matthew 6:19–21 says, "Do not store up for yourselves treasures on earth, where moth and vermin destroy, and where thieves break in and steal. But store up for yourselves treasures in heaven, where moths and vermin do not destroy, and where thieves do not break in and steal. For where your treasure is, there your heart will be also."

Prayer: Lord, you said that I should not set my heart on possessions, but set my heart on you. You promised that you would provide everything I need if I search for your kingdom first. Help me, Lord, to not fall prey to a desire for temporal possessions. Help me to seek a life filled with eternal treasures. Amen.

Scripture for further reading: Exodus 36:4–7; Philippians 4:18–20; Deuteronomy 28:9–14.

_____

_____

_____

_____

_____

_____

Greatness in Me

The world measures importance in terms of power, possession, and prestige. Jesus measures greatness in terms of service. Jesus' way is contrary to the world's way. Matthew 10:42 says, "And if anyone gives even a cup of cold water to one of these little ones who is my disciple, truly I tell you, that person will certainly not lose their reward." Worldly treasures are here today and gone tomorrow. The accurate measure of success is in the number of lives you've touched. That is an eternal treasure.

Prayer: Lord, help me to know greatness. Give me a servant's heart. Give me a heart after the things that please you. Amen.

Scripture for further reading: Joshua 22:5; Luke 12:35–48; Revelations 2:19.

_____

_____

_____

_____

_____

_____

_____

_____

_____

You Matter

If you've ever felt worthless, know that it is a lie. Satan put that idea in your head, and it is a lie. You are loved by God, the one who counts the most. Luke 12:6–7 says, "Are not five sparrows sold for two pennies? Yet not one of them is forgotten by God. Indeed, the very hairs of your head are all numbered. Don't be afraid; you are worth more than many sparrows."

Prayer: Lord, I am one with you. You are more powerful than any enemy in this world. You are an awesome God, full of splendor and beauty. You are majestic. You are wisdom and grace. What a privilege it is to walk with Almighty God. I am a living, breathing reflection of your infinite love and dominion. Amen.

Scripture for further reading: Ephesians 1:11–12; 1 Corinthians 12:14; John 3:16; Romans 8:35–39.

_____

_____

_____

_____

_____

_____

_____

_____

_____

He Chose You

God has chosen you. You are sanctified and set apart from others to know and serve our God of the universe. As royalty, your purpose is to walk in the fullness of the Spirit of unobstructed love, purity, and truth. As such, you are naturally entitled to a world of endless possibilities, a miraculous transformation from brokenness, and an overflowing abundant life. First Peter 2:9 says, "you are a chosen people, a royal priesthood, a holy nation, God's special possession, that you may declare the praises of Him who called you out of darkness into His wonderful light."

Prayer: Lord, it is a blessing to be chosen by you. As I am one with you, I am filled with infinite love. I praise you, God Almighty, ruler of heaven and earth. Your magnificence is more than I can fathom. May I serve you and fulfill the purpose for which you created me, with excellence, integrity, and righteousness. Amen.

Scripture for further reading: Ephesians 1:11–14; Romans 9:7–8; 2 Thessalonians 2:13–14.

You Are Not Working for Men

Work won't kill you, but some people just don't want to take a chance. The work you do is essential to God. But, your motivation for doing the job is even more important to Him, than the outcome. Colossians 3:23–24 says, "Whatever you do, work at it with all your heart, as working for the Lord, not for human masters, since you know that you will receive an inheritance from the Lord as a reward. It is the Lord Christ you are serving."

Prayer: Lord, my job is to care for your sheep. My job is to take care of everything you've entrusted to me. My job is to serve you. Remove my arrogance and replace it with a changed heart of humility. Help me not to put my hope in wealth, which is uncertain, but to put my faith in you, who provides everything I need for my enjoyment. Amen.

Scripture for further reading: Psalm 90:17; Proverbs 12:11; Genesis 2:15; Timothy 6:17; Proverbs 16:3.

_____

_____

_____

_____

_____

_____

_____

_____

Slackers

Slackers will find poverty. In Proverbs 14:23, we are reminded, "All hard work brings a profit, but mere talk leads only to poverty." Don't take time, resources, or energy for granted. The Bible warns against idleness. Don't be afraid to step out as your authentic self to do the work. God blesses hard work.

Prayer: Father, may I honor you by using all that you created in me and for me to maximize my full potential. May I glorify you. Make me aware of the many ways you reach out to me today. I stand in awe of the power you display in such loving ways. Amen.

Scripture for further reading: 2 Timothy 2:6; 1 Timothy 5:8; Proverbs 6:6–11; 2 Thessalonians 3:5–10.

_____

_____

_____

_____

_____

_____

_____

_____

_____

Give It Your All

Why put off until tomorrow what you can accomplish today. Well, people who procrastinate are certainly not giving it their all. God wants you to give it your all. Proverbs 13:4 confirms that "A sluggard's appetite is never filled, but the desires of the diligent are fully satisfied." Throughout the Bible, God encourages hard work and warns against idleness. Time and again, there are stories of God's reward for labor. From the beginning, when God put Adam in the Garden of Eden, He intended for him to work the land and take care of it. Even God Himself worked for six days and rested on the seventh day. Whatever you do, give it your all.

Prayer: Father, I don't want to be like the sluggard who receives nothing. I want the harvest. I feel your call for me, deep within my heart. Help me to use my work to reflect your glory. Help me to use my work to serve others, as Jesus did. Help me to do the job you set before me with diligence and excellence. Amen.

Scripture for further reading: Philippians 2:14–15; Proverbs 12:24; Proverbs 22:29; Galatians 6:9.

_____

_____

_____

_____

_____

_____

Friendship

My grandfather once told me, "Honey, to have a friend, you have to be a friend." A good friend is a gift from God. Having a friend takes effort. But it's worth it. Friends support one another, sympathize, and comfort one another. You get back what you send out — it applies to your words, your deeds, and your attitude. Proverbs 17:17 says, "A friend loves at all times."

Prayer: Lord, I thank you for godly friends. Help me never take my friends for granted, but love them as the treasures that they are. Amen.

Scripture for further reading: Proverbs 12:26; Ecclesiastes 4:9–10; Job 2:11.

Responsibility

Don't let responsibility overwhelm you. Ephesians 5:15 says, "Be very careful, then, how you live — not as unwise but as wise." The way you can do this is to include God in every aspect of your life. God is wise, loving, and all-powerful. He sets boundaries to the day and the night. He sets limits between the ocean and the shore. So, it is with setting boundaries for responsibility. God wants you to balance responsibility with rest and refreshment. If you take responsibility for people or things and don't live your life fully, that's an indication that you are making those people and things idols in your life, instead of God. The devil will lead you to believe that it's Christian to do it all and be all for others. That's a lie. God counts on you to be responsible for what He has charged you to do, not with what he's charged someone else to do for themselves. Your foot should seldom be in your neighbor's house.

Prayer: Lord, guide me to follow peace and joy. Help me set proper boundaries for my responsibilities. Thank you for this understanding. Thank you for loving me and genuinely caring about my peace and joy. I praise your Holy Name. Amen.

Scripture for further reading: Galatians 6:5; Psalm 16:5–9; Proverbs 19:19; Proverbs 25:17; Proverbs 147:14.

Don't Find Blame

When tempted to find blame, we become part of the problem instead of the solution. Romans 8:1 says, "Therefore, there is now no condemnation for those who are in Christ, Jesus." Instead of blaming, we can seek solutions. We can cover the mistakes of others. We can be a witness to the way we should go. We can pray for the grace to work out our imperfections.

Prayer: Dear Jesus, you came so that we may live life to the fullest. Forgive me when I grieve you. Instead of hardening my heart by accusing others and pointing out their errors, may I receive forgiveness and work out my imperfections. Help us focus on solutions together. Amen.

Scripture for further reading: Matthew 7:3–5; Romans 2:3; Proverbs 28:13–14.

_____

_____

_____

_____

_____

_____

_____

_____

In the Moment

Our character, developed in times of adversity, matters to God. You find out what kind of person you are when faced with trials and tribulations. So, pay attention to your response when challenged. Do you share hope or disillusionment; do you model love or anger; or, do you respond in bitterness or kindness? Matthew 10:16 says, "I am sending you out like sheep among wolves. Therefore, be as shrewd as snakes and as innocent as doves."

Prayer: God, thank you for joy, even during trials. Even during trials, there is beauty to behold, joy to be had, kindness to share, and wisdom to understand. Help me maximize the moment. During trials Father, remind me to notice the blessings of the moment, so that I don't give power to the problem; instead I will give power to the glory all around me. In Jesus' name, I pray. Amen.

Scripture for further reading: Galatians 6:7–9; 2 Peter 3:18; Hebrews 6:1.

It Only Takes One Person

It is incredible to think of the influence one person can have to make a difference in the world. Only one man, Martin Luther King, gave hope to a nation of persecuted blacks. Only one woman, Mother Teresa, spoke out to give dignity to those in poverty. You can make a difference in the life of others. You have a circle of influence in your home, with friends, in your community, and within the world. Matthew 5:14–16 says, "You are the light of the world…Let your light shine before others that they may see your good deeds and glorify your Father in heaven." Give voice to those who have none.

Prayer: Lord, there are so many times that I see injustice and think, "What can I do? I'm just one person." When I think defeating thoughts, help me remember that you put terrific people in the world, with ordinary talents, and ordinary skill, to do amazing things. When I see injustice, I can do something. When I do what I can, I can trust you to do the rest. Thank you, Lord, that you made me in your image and that you created me for such a time as this. Amen.

Scripture for further reading: James 5:20; 1 Corinthians 9:22; Ephesians 2:10.

_____

_____

_____

_____

_____

_____

Change

One of the most profound sayings was from a Greek philosopher named Heraclitus, around 500 BC. He said, "Change is the only constant in life." People's reaction to change is the same now as it was then. At times, we get caught up in the busyness of life just to keep up with it all. Other times, we get so settled in our ways, we fight change. But Heraclitus missed the main point: while life is truly always changing, the one constant is God. He is the same today as He was yesterday, and He'll be the same tomorrow. God never changes. To get direction through changing times, we are best served by letting God be our guide. First John 5:5 says, "Who is it that overcomes the world? Only the one who believes that Jesus is the Son of God."

Prayer: Father, change is everywhere. I confess, sometimes I am an advocate of reform. Other times, busyness consumes me. When exhausted by change, I tend to hold on tightly, not wanting to change. No matter what change brings, help me continue to do good and trust in you. I don't know what tomorrow brings, but I know the one who does. Because of you, I can remain peaceful through it all. No matter what change brings, I can face it, make it, and enjoy it. God, I know you are on my side. Amen.

Scripture for further reading: 2 Thessalonians 2:11–15; James 4:13–17; Proverbs 27:1.

_____

_____

_____

_____

_____

Grace, Grace, and More Grace

When you open the door for God to work in your life, you can expect miracles. God gives strength when you feel weak. God softens hearts, once hardened. God has the right words when it seems there are none. God makes a way when all seems lost. Nothing is too hard for Him. Lamentations 3:22–24 says, "Because of the Lord's great love, we are not consumed, for His compassions never fail. They are new every morning; great is your faithfulness. I say to myself, 'The Lord is my portion; therefore I will wait for Him.'"

Prayer: Forgive me, Lord, when I dare to think I have all the answers. My understanding is limited. When I try to take control to fix things, I am like a toddler trying to tie my shoes for the first time. Instead of asking Daddy to help me, I insist on doing it myself. Forgive me when I don't include you, seek you, and trust you for the answer. Because of your grace, I can let go, stop worrying, stop wearing myself out, and turn everything over to you, my Lord and Savior. Instead, I can go forward in joy and victory, knowing that God has it under control. I pray for grace, grace, and more grace, Lord. I praise your Holy Name. Amen.

Scripture for further reading: Ephesians 1:3–10; Deuteronomy 10:21; Exodus 15:26; Jeremiah 32:27.

_____

_____

_____

_____

_____

Radiant Life

Time is a fantastic resource. I've heard both sayings, "there's never enough time," and "there is time enough." I don't know which is true: "this is a perfect time," or "there's never a perfect time." Does "everything get better with time," or "Does time heal nothing?" What makes the difference between the good and bad times? One thing is certain, and that is, God does not change. "God, who is enthroned from of old, does not change" (Psalm 55:19). He is the same through all times. He is the same yesterday, today, and tomorrow. Throughout all time, God is magnificent and radiant.

Prayer: Help me, Lord, to spend time wisely. May the knowledge of who you are, and who I am in you, fill my spirit. With the time I am given, may I perpetuate your love, power, joy, and fullness of life. All honor and glory are yours, God. Amen.

Scripture for further reading: 2 Corinthians 4:8–11; 2 Timothy 1:7; 1 John 4:18.

_____

_____

_____

_____

_____

_____

_____

_____

Every Day Blessings

Hebrews 2:4 reminds us that God distributes, "according to His will." Why doesn't He distribute equally to everyone? Here's what I believe to be true: God tells us to enter His gates in thanksgiving. Do you give Him thanks for the miracles of today? We have so much to be thankful for. Those who are deaf would be filled with wonder to hear the sparrow's morning song or the laughter of a child. Many elders understand the miracle of days when we can do something as simple as jump out of bed. Be thankful for every mercy and every miracle of the day, and say so. Then watch what happens.

Prayer: Dear God, you bless me greatly. My daughter thanked me for a toy that I gave her. She appreciated it so much; it made me want to buy her more. Another time, she threw her toy down and expressed disappointment that it wasn't what she wanted. It made me think twice about purchasing another toy any time soon. So, it is with you, Lord. Thank you for the miracles of today. Help me name them one by one. I praise you for every good thing in my life. I praise your Holy Name. Amen.

Scripture for further reading: Galatians 3:1–5; Acts 3:16; Acts 19:11; Psalm 77:14.

_____

_____

_____

_____

_____

_____

There's Someone at the Door

The world can tear you apart when you rely only on your abilities to fight your battles. God is strength and a refuge for those who open the doors of their hearts to receive Him. In Revelation 3:20, Jesus promised, "Here I am. I stand at the door and knock. If anyone hears my voice and opens the door, I will come in and eat with that person, and they with me." Open the door of your heart and let Him into your life. God will deliver your needs. Celebrate Him.

Prayer: Father, I know that I am capable of many things, but I can do all things with you. Thank you for your incredible power at work in my life. I rejoice in you. Thank you, Lord Jesus. Amen.

Scripture for further reading: Psalm 46:1–3; 1 Corinthians 4:10; Psalm 40:17; Psalm 63:7.

Grandma

No one ever understood my Grandma — she was odd — a "Jesus fanatic," they would say. But she was always kind and gentle. She had a good heart and a peaceful spirit. When bad things happened, she was patient. She always put her faith and trust in God. She always seemed to be joyful, even in the smallest things, like butterflies and hummingbirds. My grandma never told me about the fruits of the Holy Spirit, which are love, peace, joy, goodness, kindness, gentleness, self-discipline, patience, and faithfulness. She showed me what these were. Matthew 5:10–12 says, "Blessed are those who are persecuted because of righteousness, for theirs is the kingdom of heaven. Blessed are you when people insult you," I pray that I grow up to be like Grandma.

Prayer: Lord, when people revile and persecute me and say all kinds of evil against me falsely for Christ's sake, let me be exceedingly glad, for great is my reward in heaven. Amen.

Scripture for further reading: Galatians 5:22–23; 1 John 4:16; Ephesians 3:16–17; Ephesians 4:2; 2 Corinthians 6:6–7.

No Doubting Thomas

Many things block the flow of God's blessings in your life: pride, lust, greed, unforgiveness, just to name a few. God will forgive all your sins if you name them. Ask Him to forgive you and seek His holy presence. He'll show you a better way. In 1 Peter 3:12, it says, "For the eyes of the Lord are on the righteous, and His ears are attentive to their prayer," Partnered with faith, the power of a pure heart is beneficial.

Prayer: Lord, teach me how to pray. If there is anything in me that is not pleasing, reveal it to me, Lord, as much as I can bear, so that I may receive forgiveness. Cleanse my heart. Help me to pray in faith, with no doubting. Give me a pure heart and confidence to believe and trust in you. Amen.

Scripture for further reading: James 1:6; James 5:14–16; James 14:16; Romans 8:26–27; Matthew 21:21.

_____

_____

_____

_____

_____

_____

_____

_____

_____

_____

The Answer to Your Prayers

Do you ever think that God doesn't hear your prayers? Well, He does. He may say, "Yes." He may say, "Not now," or He may say, "No. There's better in store for you." But you can be sure that He has heard your prayer. Whatever the answer, it will always be for the very best outcome. Deuteronomy 4:7 says, "What other nation is so great as to have their gods near them the way the Lord our God is near us whenever we pray to Him?"

Prayer: Lord Father, sometimes my prayers seem unanswered. Help me to remember there is something more in store for me. May I abide in you daily; my prayer is for your will. Only then can I be confident for answered prayers. Keep my motives pure. Prayers of a sinner, and prayers for my pleasure, are not pleasing to you and won't be answered. When I pray, give me a pure heart, pure motives, and a desire for your will. I pray this in Jesus' holy name. Amen.

Scripture for further reading: John 5:14–15; John 15:1–11; Isaiah 1:15; 1 Peter 3:12; Matthew 6:9–13; James 4:3.

_____

_____

_____

_____

_____

_____

_____

_____

Living for God

Who are you living for; yourself, or God? God will give you what you need if you choose to live for Him. Real joy only comes once you've completely committed yourself to Jesus Christ. Jesus is waiting for you to invite Him into your life. In Acts 26:18, Jesus reminds us, "to open their eyes and turn them from darkness to light, and from the power of Satan to God, so that they may receive forgiveness of sins and a place among those who are sanctified by faith in me."

Prayer: Jesus, I believe in you and receive you in my life. Help me to live a life that is pleasing to you. You saved us and paid the price for our sins. My confidence is in you, Lord Jesus. Amen.

Scripture for further reading: 1 Thessalonians 2:2–8; Galatians 1:10; Romans 14:8.

_____

_____

_____

_____

_____

_____

_____

_____

_____

Believe and Receive

Romans 11:36 says, "For from Him and through Him and for Him are all things. To Him be the glory forever. Amen." Know that God loves you and has chosen you to be in a relationship with Him. Then, receive Him into your life and accept eternal life and joy.

Prayer: Lord, I know that no matter how angry, depressed, or hurt I feel, your love will never let me go. Help me to be less self-absorbed and more aware of the strength and courage available, through you, to face the day. I believe in you, and I receive and accept your love, power, and glory. Thank you for this blessing. Amen.

Scripture for further reading: John 3:14–17; Ephesians 1:15–22; Ephesians 3:14–21; 2 Corinthians 5:21.

_____

_____

_____

_____

_____

_____

_____

_____

_____

Enjoy Every Good Thing God Has to Offer

Enjoy the good things that are here, while on this earth. The universe is your playground. Everything that exists has its beauty or lesson. Everything God has created leaves an imprint on our souls. The mountains display majesty, lakes instill tranquility, and flowers inspire beauty. Isaiah 51:15 reminds us of the One who created all the beauty in the world, "For I am the Lord your God, who stirs up the sea so that its waves roar — the Lord Almighty is His name."

Prayer: Father, every good and perfect gift is from you. Thank you for the blessings of joy, rest, and beauty. May I enjoy, appreciate, and give thanks to you, for you are good. Amen.

Scripture for further reading: Psalm 103:2; Psalm 136:26; Numbers 17:8; Numbers 6:24–25; Song of Songs 2:12; Song of Songs 4:16.

DECEMBER 22

Humility Is the Ladder to Divine Understanding

Humility is a prominent Christian virtue. It is a state of mind that is pleasing to God. Christ was an example of humility. God promises honor to those who are humble. Proverbs 1:33 says, "humility comes before honor." But this seems like a paradox. How can humility bring honor and greatness? It is easy to understand when you consider how people respond to others who are kind and gentle, compared to those who are rude and arrogant. When you are generous and modest, people are more inclined to treat you with honor and greatness.

Prayer: Father, teach me to be kind and gentle instead of rude and arrogant. I am not attracted to people who are prideful and I don't want to act that way myself. Teach me to be a better example of humility. Help me to let go of pride. I ask this through your Son, Jesus, who stands by my side and waits. Amen.

Scripture for further reading: Proverbs 16:19; 1 Corinthians 13:4; Ezekiel 16:49; Ephesians 4:2.

_____

_____

_____

_____

_____

_____

Perilous Pride

Pride is a dangerous thing. If anything causes you to think more highly of yourself than you ought to, it is perilous. Ego acts smug, self-important, and stubborn. It will destroy relations with God and friends faster than anything. Proverbs 8:13 says, "I hate pride and arrogance, evil behavior and perverse speech."

Prayer: Lord, teach me to be patient with others, and protect me from pride. Remove my arrogance and replace it with a heart of humility. Amen.

Scripture for further reading: 2 Corinthians 10:12–13; 2 Timothy 3:1–5; James 4:10; Psalm 10:4.

_____

_____

_____

_____

_____

_____

_____

_____

_____

_____

_____

Living Dangerous

The Bible says that anytime we are prideful, we are living in opposition to God. When we are prideful, it blocks God's grace in our lives. That is a foolish and risky way to live. James 4:6 says, "God opposes the proud but shows grace to the humble." Pride is repugnant to God. It is the practice of stealing glory that rightly belongs to Him. Pride hinders us from experiencing the beauty inherent in having an intimate relationship with Him. It's appropriate to value accomplishments but dangerous in large quantities. To fight pride, it helps to force yourself to listen more than you talk, seek feedback, and ask questions instead of always offering your opinion. Remember where you got the skill, talent, and opportunity to succeed, and always give God the glory.

Prayer: Help me, Lord, to be an example of your grace. Although I start with good intentions, I wind up falling short. When I am prideful, I don't reflect your beauty to those around me. Help me to change my heart. Amen.

Scripture for further reading: 2 Corinthians 10:14–18; Proverbs 16:18; Proverbs 21:24; Proverbs 27:2; Isaiah 13:11.

_____

_____

_____

_____

_____

_____

Don't Miss Out

"The angel said to [Mary], 'Do not be afraid. Mary, you have found favor with God. You will conceive and give birth to a son, and you are to call Him Jesus. He will be great and will be called the Son of the Most High. The Lord God will give Him the throne of His father David." (Luke 1:30–32). These are comforting words. The details of Jesus' birth also teach us about the nature of people. People at that time thought that the Messiah would be someone of position and power, someone who would save them from Roman rulers. The Messiah, however, was born into lowly circumstances — his parents had neither position nor power. People were so focused on a worldly status that they missed the Savior when He came. Today, is it any different? Don't miss God, focused on the busyness of this holiday season. It's not too late. Start now, thanking God for His unparalleled gift.

Prayer: Lord, in your immense love, you sent Christ to be flesh among us. In your mercy, those of us who believe in Christ receive eternal life. All honor and glory are yours forever. Help me recognize how I can to bring relief, shelter, food, and health for all those in need on this blessed day. Amen.

Scripture for further reading: 2 Corinthians 9:15; John 1:14; 1 Timothy 1:5–17.

_____

_____

_____

_____

_____

Hope for Our Nation

Has anyone throughout universal history been made holy by criticizing or judging others? You are not helping yourself or anyone else by being judgmental or critical. "Search me, God, and know my heart; test me and know my anxious thoughts. See if there is any offensive way in me, and lead me in the way everlasting" (Psalms 139:23–24). There has never been a greater time of need in our country for the faithful to confess their sins and pray for our nation's healing. It is hope for our nation when those in authority take hold of the strength, courage, and wisdom available through God's Word. May we be a blessed nation whose God is our Lord.

Prayer: Lord, I pray that you will restore our nation and give us hope for the future. Give those in authority, the wisdom to hear and follow you. Bring an awakening so that many will come to know Jesus. I pray for wise counsel and true leadership. I pray for protection against worldly risks. I pray for your hand to restore faith and family for all those who are without it. Search my heart Lord and lead me in the everlasting way. Amen.

Scripture for further reading: Isaiah 33:6; Psalm 33:12; 2 Chronicles 7:14; Matthew 12:21; 1Timothy 2:1.

Changed Life: Sweeter Than Honey

There are too many children raised in dysfunctional families. My childhood had its own kind of turmoil. In the search for something pure, sweet, and beautiful, I found the word of God. It touched my heart and gave me hope for something better. Psalm 119:103–104 says, "How sweet are your words to my taste, sweeter than honey to my mouth. I gain understanding from your precepts; therefore, I hate every wrong path."

Prayer: Lord, I wait expectantly for your splendor to take shape in my life. Set me on the path of your choosing. I will, with your help, replace lack, tears, anguish, sadness, and negativity with gladness, love, success, joy, and peace. I continually experience your incredible blessings. As I trust you, I witness and cherish the glory of your enthralling presence. Amen.

Scripture for further reading: Colossians 3:10; John 5:41–44; Psalm 51:10–12; 1 John 3:2–3; 1 Peter 2:9.

_____

_____

_____

_____

_____

_____

_____

_____

No Better Friend Than Jesus

Not everyone who calls himself a Christian will go to heaven. Matthew 7:14 says, "But small is the gate and narrow the road that leads to life, and only a few find it." Jesus wants a relationship with all of us, even though we are not perfect. Those who admit their shortcomings will receive His grace and forgiveness. If you know someone without a relationship with God, do three things for them. First, pray for them. Next, baptize them, and finally, teach them to obey everything Christ has commanded. God will be with you and provide you with everything you need to complete the task. Is God asking you to share your faith with someone today?

Prayer: Lord, I pray that people of integrity, all over this world, stand up to fulfill your calling. I pray that our children will see us as examples of dedicated people committed to following you. Amen.

Scripture for further reading: Luke 8:4–15; 1 Thessalonians 5:19–22; John 15:1–2.

_____

_____

_____

_____

_____

_____

_____

Guard Your Heart

Proverbs 15:13 says, "A happy heart makes the face cheerful, but heartache crushes the spirit." Be gentle with people's hearts, including your own. Be very selective about whom you allow to touch your life. You are a precious child of God and sacred beyond compare.

Prayer: Lord, I pray that longstanding offenses will be healed and forgiven. May Christians demonstrate honor and act in your reconciling power. You are the only hope for deep-seated heartache. I pray that all those who suffer, overcome through the power and blood of Jesus Christ. Amen.

Scripture for further reading: Proverbs 2:7–8; Proverbs 4:20–27; Psalm 119:9.

_____

_____

_____

_____

_____

_____

_____

_____

_____

_____

Healer of My Soul

Some people won't allow themselves to love others, for fear of heartache. The truth is, love leaves us vulnerable. Building a barricade is like solitary confinement. It is a self-inflicted prison and an assault on the soul. Forgiveness opens the prison door that releases us to give and receive love. That is freedom. Love is powerful, breathtaking, and exhilarating all at the same time. Seek God to help you forgive. Ask God to open your heart to experience all the blessings that love can bring. Psalm 147:3 says, "He heals the brokenhearted and binds up their wounds."

Prayer: Lord, I pray for the healing of broken relationships. I pray for comfort to all those who are suffering from a broken heart. I pray that you will grant the glorious blessing of love for all those who come to know and serve you. Amen.

Scripture for further reading: Psalm 30:2; Psalm 34:17–22; Romans 8:28.

We Are Set Apart

Second Corinthians 6:14–18 says, "Do not be yoked together with unbelievers. For what do righteousness and wickedness have in common? Or what fellowship can light have with darkness? What harmony is there between Christ and Belial? What does a believer have in common with an unbeliever? What agreement is there between the temple of God and idols? For we are the temple of the living God. As God said: 'I will live with them and walk among them, and I will be their God, and they will be my people.'" So many times, in the Bible, we're instructed to be with unbelievers and share the good news of Christ. It is good to lead others to Christ if you are influencing them, and they are not infecting you. You are responsible for guarding your heart and keeping yourself from being polluted by the world. Pray for wisdom and discernment.

Prayer: Lord, I pray for wisdom and discernment. I pray to be the example that leads others to you. Help me to be continually assess whether I'm influencing others or compromising my ways. Help me to be an excellent example of your love, goodness, kindness, gentleness, self-control, peace, joy, faithfulness, and patience. In Jesus' name, I pray. Amen.

Scripture for further reading: 1 Thessalonians 1:2–7; 1 Thessalonians 5:12–15; 1 Thessalonians 5:23–24.

Printed in the United States
By Bookmasters